G. H. Elliott.

The bad food guide

The bad food guide

by Derek Cooper
illustrated by
Michael Foreman

Routledge and Kegan Paul   London

First published 1967
by Routledge & Kegan Paul Ltd
Broadway House, 68–74 Carter Lane
London, E.C.4

Printed in Great Britain
by Cox & Wyman Ltd
London, Reading and Fakenham

Contents

This book had its origin in a talk given in the B.B.C.'s
'Today' programme in September 1965. It was subsequently
reprinted in *The Listener*. Colin Franklin of Routledge &
Kegan Paul saw the piece and asked me to expand it.
I would like to thank all those members of the catering
industry who were good enough to discuss their work with me
and I respect the desire of some of them for anonymity.
I am particularly grateful to Joseph McCullough, Michael
Fitzpatrick and Desmond Ryan who gave me a lot of helpful
advice in the early stages of preparing the book. I found *The
Englishman's Food* by J. C. Drummond and Anne Wilbraham,
the recently published book by John Burnett *Plenty and
Want*, *The British Eating Out* a report from Britain's National
Catering Inquiry, sponsored by Smethursts Food Limited
and *The Foods We Eat*, a survey of meals undertaken by
the Market Division of W. S. Crawford Limited, most useful.
This England (1960–65) provided some of the more eccentric
quotations, but my main source of inspiration (apart from
several profitable visits to Hotelympia 1966 where I reaped a
rich harvest of information not normally available to someone
writing a book like this), has been in the pages of the
trade press which are required reading for anybody who
wants to know what's going on behind the scenes. *The Hotel
and Catering Times* (every Thursday 6d), *The Hotel and Catering
Review* (first Thursday of each month 2s 6d) and *The
Caterer and Hotelkeeper* (every Thursday 1s 6d) are the three
most useful.
The following people gave me information, help and
constructive advice: R. S. Anand, K. P. Armitage, Joy
Barnett, Mary Button, D. Cameron, M. Coomaraswamy,
Yves Delany, Jay Dick, Gordon Dudley-Browne, Ina Everton,
F. C. Ewing, Jolyon Fisher, Helmut Fisk, Carys Ford,
N. Foy, Bernice Friedman, William Gay, S. K. Guan,

Fred Green, R. E. Greene, Alfie Hall, Gerard Hans, A. W. Hampton, Desmond Hopkinson, Martin Hutton, I. Jacobs, Major Simon Jago, David H. Jones, Glyn Jones, S. P. R. King, Elizabeth King, J. S. Kant, A. Kruger, Jimmy Kwong, Herman Levy, N. Lucas, John MacInnes, Stuart Mackenzie, Michael Nightingale, Conor O'Brien, Taz Onazi, Bunny Padmore, Derek Palmer, K. S. Petrides, Harold Rabin, Nigel S. Reynolds, Neil Rhind, Anthony Schooling, Dancy Smith, Alice Somiah, Soon Whatt Siang, G. C. Struys, Pillai Sundaram, Romaine Timaeus, Clee Tracey, Paul Vaughan, David Walker, Ben Wood.

Finally, as much of this book has been compiled from my own experience in various parts of Britain, I must record a very special debt to those workers in the industry, who, through their slovenliness, inexpertise, lack of hygiene, dishonesty, rudeness and apathy have given chapter and verse to large chunks of what follows.

Introduction

'The destiny of nations depends on the manner in which they eat'

Brillat-Savarin

There are plenty of books about good food. This is a
book about bad food. Badly prepared food, badly cooked
food, food badly served in bad surroundings. Bad? Bad
meaning in this context not good enough. Bad meaning
inferior, inadequate, indigestible, pretentious, tasteless,
uneatable, uninspired, monotonous, unappetising. We
Britons are internationally famous for our gardens, our dogs,
our beer, our cloth, our cars, our villages, our whisky, our
public schools, our monarchy, our democratic institutions,
our cricket – umpteen books have been written explaining
their glories to those unfortunate enough to have been born
outside these islands. But nobody has yet written a book
about the bad food for which we are equally famous
overseas.

Although the mass of people in Britain are eating
better than ever before, that isn't saying much. Our
reputation for bad food is not a phenomenon special to
this century. For the poor there never was a time of good
living and yet emotionally we like to believe there was some
distant past when rosy-cheeked women and strapping
men in smocks lived off the fat of the land. The current
piece of advertising by a pork-pie manufacturer reads,
'Harris bring back the golden age of English food'. They
date it to around 1770 when they produced their first pie
which sounds reasonable if you don't examine the claim
too closely. And yet Charles Moritz, a Swiss who
visited England in the 1780's, saw no signs of this Golden
Age. He described the average Englishman's mid-day meal
of that time as, 'a piece of half-boiled or half-roasted meat;
and a few cabbage-leaves, boiled in plain water'.

Perhaps the Golden Age was in Dickens' time? Again,
examination doesn't bear this out. Dickens may have
romanticized the blow-outs of his youth, but in the 1850's
when Dickens was at the height of his powers, the reality
was a very different one of chronic poverty and acute hunger.
The way in which the average meal was prepared was –

if contemporary accounts can be believed – nothing on which to look back with envy. In *The Memories of a Stomach* published in the 1850's there occurs this tribute: 'The English system of cooking would be impertinent for me to describe; but still when I think of that huge mound of parboiled ox-flesh, with sodden dumplings, floating in a saline, greasy mixture, surrounded by carrots looking red with disgust, and turnips pale with dismay, I cannot help a sort of inward shudder and making comparisons unfavourable to English gastronomy.' So you see, we're not exactly novices in the art of bad food.

Because of the very stringent libel laws in Britain, this book is factual where it can be, but where I would have given specific examples of actual establishments I have had to present them (by altering names, location and other details) as 'imaginary'. They are, of course, far from being a figment of the imagination – they all too unhappily exist.

You will find no mention in this book of the hundreds of hotels, restaurants and inns where it is possible to get good food, well cooked at reasonable prices. As the Director of the British Hotels and Restaurants Association personally assured me, there are already plenty of books about good food. Nor does this book record the virtues of all the good hoteliers, restaurateurs, chefs and waiters. They have helped to give British food its growing reputation for isolated excellences, and we ought to be grateful to them. Their praises are sung extensively in *The Good Food Guide* and by food and wine writers whose pleasure it is to harp on the good things of life, not the bad.

I am concerned with the seamier side of eating out and, above all, with the revolution that has taken place in the last few years. More money in circulation has meant that more and more people have been able to afford to eat out. The enormous technological changes in food production have been reflected in a greater move towards standardization.

Before the war you could find the same tinned baked beans or tinned peas in cafés from Land's End to John O'Groats. But now standardization is even more in evidence. Through the miracle of deep-freeze scampi has been spread like manna from Southend to Stornoway. The reverence which this tasteless food commands is deeply symptomatic of the contemporary debasement of taste. In the organizational side of the industry the move has again been to standardization. Hotels and inns have gradually fallen out of private ownership into the hands of large chains, some good, some bad. The extension of franchise catering, whereby semi-skilled staff serve food supplied to them from a central depôt means that one gets exactly the same Quikburger in Glasgow that one gets in Oxford Street. The era of technical development that the catering industry in Britain is undergoing will inevitably mean even more standardization. Less and less food will be cooked in the kitchens of small restaurants, and more and more will be prepared in factories under conditions of the utmost hygiene, and deep-frozen for consumption hundreds of miles away and months later. The scientific production of eggs, chickens, and veal will inevitably be extended to other animal products with what many feel will be a corresponding loss of flavour and nutrition.

This standardization is not necessarily going to mean that the food will be badly cooked but it will mean that it will have a uniform blandness, what I describe as 'untaste'.

The first requirement of mass catering is to produce a product that is going to be acceptable to as many people as possible and, therefore, the less taste or flavour a product has, the less likely it is to be rejected as being too spicy, or too sweet, or too salty. The move towards blandness has been so gradual over the years that we have now come to accept the almost complete absence of taste and flavour from a large range of processed foods. We have lost our skill with herbs and spices to such an extent that we find most foreign food totally unacceptable. Hence, the great summer processions of Dormobiles bound for Italy and Spain laden with cardboard boxes of tinned, tasteless and therefore preferred food.

There is no doubt that there is a renascent interest in good food in Britain. More cookery books are sold than ever before. No self-respecting Hampstead housewife is without her own pâté recipe. But when you come to examine the great lumpen catering product, very little of this minority enthusiasm is reflected in the daily round of custard and chips.

It is all too easy to regard London as the norm for catering. Central and outer London has the remarkably high number of 227 hotels, restaurants and inns which qualify for inclusion in *The Good Food Guide*. But although London is Britain's first city, it is not Britain. Let us look at Britain's *second* city. Birmingham has a population of over a million. I find it sadly significant that while London has 227 good places to eat, Birmingham has *six*. Of these one is Indian and another run by students at the College of Food and Domestic Arts.

It's not the function of this book to apportion blame for our long tradition of bad food. I think the responsibility rests not with the industry itself, but with the people they are catering for. I have the utmost sympathy for caterers who are trying hard to do a self-respecting job in the face of almost universal indifference. If the people of Birmingham were prepared to support 20 or 30 good restaurants, they would very soon get them. Apparently they are not.

There is, alas, no reason for optimism on the eating front. For the minority prepared to pay for the privilege there will always be a small number of good restaurants. The majority of us will continue to put up uncomplainingly, perhaps even with a sort of masochistic pleasure, with the kind of bad food and bad service that is described in the following fourteen chapters. If M. Brillat-Savarin was right, our national destiny is a dim one indeed!

Pride and prejudice

'I find it very English that not only do you have this food, but that you have also a sort of triumph about it – you know, people really do like it being so awful'

French Diplomat – off duty

Let's face it, food is not something you talk about. As a nation we find the eating business rather embarrassing. That's why we've tried to give the impression that the whole process is half humorous, half debasing. The names of our favourite dishes are somehow comic: chips, mash, tripe, pud. We don't roll the words round our mouths, we've made them as stark and ugly as possible: nosh, snack, blow out, grub, tack, spread. What we do with our food is equally crude and brutal: we bolt, crunch, scoff, chew, gnaw, gulp, champ, lick, pick and peck it. And when we're drinking we swill, suck, swig, sip and soak it. If our food vocabulary is nasty, brutish and short, we've made amends in other ways. We've learnt to live with our food by laughing at it.

A comedian has only got to stand his hair on end, climb into a baggy suit and start talking about food to have us in convulsions. A mention of kippers, cabbage, bubble and squeak, custard or cockles and we're rolling about. The mere suggestion of a delicacy like Eccles cake, cow heel, crumpet, Bath bun, faggots or haggis, and strong men have to march up and down the aisles restoring order.

Are we laughing at ourselves or at the food, or are we so inhibited by the apparatus of eating that our laughter is a kind of tribal release? When we come to talk about food face to face, there's an element of shame in the air, of resignation:

SHE   Will you want any supper, then?

HE   Well, we had a big tea, didn't we?

SHE   Yes, we had a big tea.

HE   I don't mind really.

SHE   Well, it's up to you. I can't settle till we've had it.

HE   We may as well get it over then.

SHE   Get it out of the way . . . .

HE   We shouldn't be hungry really. We had a big breakfast.

SHE   And look at all that pudding you had, and you ate that Swiss roll, too.

HE   Yes, but you finished the trifle.
SHE   Well, I'll see what I can find.
HE   Yes, anything will do. Don't put yourself out.
SHE   I might open a tin then?
HE   Yes, a small tin of something, that would do.
SHE   We don't want much.

Note the overtones of guilt, the acceptance that although
eating is a base function – a kind of refuelling – stuffing
oneself overfull can be a symptom of moral degeneration.
There's also the recognition that eating is part of life's
unwelcome routine, like getting up, and washing.
All these prejudices are still very much a part of our national
Puritan heritage. When it comes to public honours, people
connected with cooking food are conveniently forgotten or
fobbed off with some minor distinction. In the 1966 New
Year Honours, Raymond Postgate (Public Stomach Number
One) was awarded the O.B.E. To put the rôle of gastronomy
in its proper place, however, Brian Statham, a cricketer, was
awarded the higher distinction of a C.B.E. Thank God, even
though we've long since lost the British Empire, we can still
put its officers in their right and proper order of precedence.
I think we once did give a cook an M.B.E., but he must have
rescued some animal from drowning to deserve it. Two of
London's outstanding chefs were honoured recently, but
not by us. Marius Dutruy was promoted to be an officer of
the Legion d'Honneur, and Georges Pannier was made
Chevalier de Merité Agricole.
It's no wonder that by 1970 there'll be a shortage of 300,000
workers in the catering industry in Britain. Our record in
the international field is equally unimpressive. When the 1965
International Gastronomic Festival was held in Stuttgart,
there were 400 entrants from all over the world. The only
British competitors were a Cornish hotelier and his two
foreign chefs. They ought to get a medal for 'outstanding
perseverance in the face of national apathy'. At the time of

writing Britain still remains unrepresented in the World Federation of Culinary Societies.

Mind you, we don't get much of a lead from those in public life. Mr. Harold Wilson's sole preference seems to be for bottled sauce made in a factory and there's not much encouragement, gastronomically, from the Palace either. Mrs McKee, who cooked for the Queen Mother and Princess Margaret, has claimed: 'Apart from being told to curtsey whenever I saw Her Royal Highness, and to avoid the use of garlic, nobody told me how to behave or what to cook when I first joined the present Queen and her husband at Clarence House'. In fairness to Mrs McKee, one ought to add that after a bit she did 'forget' about the veto on garlic and from then on, as there were no complaints, she continued to use 'traces of garlic in cooking undetected'. Following Mrs McKee's culinary adventures with the Royal Family is almost like reading an Agatha Christie novel. One wonders how long she's going to get away with it, because as a recent report in the magazine *Today* revealed, the Royal tastebuds are among the most highly trained in the world:

'Where so many people are mistaken is in supposing that the Royal palate is exotic – that the Queen breakfasts on caviare, lunches on larks' tongues and dines on filleted porcupine. In point of fact, her tastes are quite simple. She is not fond of any shell fish, but has a weakness for game and venison, particularly if it is shot by a member of the Royal circle. As she has said: "It tastes so much better then".'

And that is quite remarkable. I doubt whether even the great Escoffier's powers of discrimination extended to the point of slaughter. For activity involving horses or dogs or shooting, the Royal Family is always news but, when it comes to eating, the gossip columnists have a thin time, although it does seem the Royals go in for extremes. The

5

Daily Sketch, some time ago, printed the following piece of tabletalk:

'We told you on Tuesday of the Queen's preference for large table napkins. Today we report Princess Margaret's preference for tiny knives and forks. For when the Princess eats at Kensington Palace, specially small tableware is laid for her. She uses a cheese knife for a dinner knife and tea-forks as dessert forks.'

It's well within the tradition of British reticence that we shouldn't know too much about what Royalty eat. Information about their outsize napkins or tiny forks could hardly be described as *lèse-majesté*.

Anyway in Britain what you eat is often the least important aspect of a meal. I was having a meal once with three other people in a hotel in Yorkshire. Halfway through the meal I realized that the person opposite, who had in fact ordered roast duck, was eating cold ham. 'I thought you asked for duck,' I said. 'Well, I did, but this is just as nice,' was the disarming reply.

Not minding about food has become a national obsession and it's difficult not to find oneself in sympathy with the honest restaurateur who slowly and inexorably becomes saddened and corrupted by the willingness of his clients to accept everything uncomplainingly.

I'm quite convinced that almost every man and woman who goes into catering does so with the best intentions: to give really good food, really good service, at reasonable prices. When they find, to their surprise, that their customers can't tell the difference between well cooked food and badly cooked food, that they don't mind what is put before them, that they don't seem to object if one waiter does the work of six and that they seldom dispute the price, however exorbitant, only the most strongminded survive with their integrity intact.

But even in England there are thresholds of misery beyond which the average person won't go. Not long ago, patients in a Watford hospital went on a hunger strike. They arranged to have food smuggled in, and then began cooking eggs and steak and chips in the hospital kitchen. The bedridden had hot meals brought in from outside in plastic containers. This is perhaps not surprising when one finds out how little is spent on patients in our hospitals. One catering officer in the South of England recently described how he could feed a patient for 3s 6d a day! Which may account for the strange condition found by the Nuffield Provincial Hospitals Trust when in 1963 they took a clinical look at food in 152 British hospitals. They claimed that nearly half the food prepared went back uneaten, there was scant attention paid to patients' nutritional requirements and that some hospital kitchens were so insanitary that they would qualify for prosecution if they were found in commercial establishments. The report was compiled by three nutritionists at the London School of

Hygiene and Tropical Medicine. They recorded that the total waste of food in hospitals has been estimated at between £44 and £56 million a year.

They found that the conditions I've just described at Watford were not unique. Patients tended frequently to rely on biscuits, sweets, fruit and soft drinks being brought in by their relatives. In fact some hospitals have a rule that fruit should not be supplied because enough will probably be brought in from outside.

But there are certain classes in Britain who do put up with totally wretched food day after day primarily, I believe, because they have been brought up to believe that food tastes like that any way, and there's not much you can do about it. I'm referring to that floating male population who still keep alive by eating in London's drearier clubs. An American writer, who'd been entertained to lunch by a peer in one of these places, rang me up later in the day and asked if it was some kind of terrible joke. 'Nobody can seriously eat like that – I mean, it must be a kind of hoax?' He'd been given oxtail soup, a tiny burnt lamb chop, cabbage, carrots, boiled potatoes and rice pudding.

I then explained to him, in some detail, that he had been eating exactly the same kind of food that is habitually consumed in British preparatory and public schools. Most of of the men with power and money in this country were fed this kind of diet for their twelve most formative years. Quite naturally, the clubs, which are an extension of the monastic life of school, afford a splendid opportunity to recreate the jolly times of bygone boyhood. As the food isn't very nice, there's no temptation to fall into a state of disgrace by actually enjoying it.

In Britain we like to think we have a healthy and balanced attitude to food – we're not *obsessed* with it. We spend more time in our gardens than in our kitchens; we spend our money not on eating well, but on decorating our homes, on crazy-paving and three-piece suites. But the obsession with home can have its side effects on the stomach, as a recent letter in *Weekend* revealed:

'For years, my husband and I have kept our food bills to bare necessities to save money for the deposit on a house of our own. At last we have moved into the house of our dreams, but we are still living on a diet of milk and biscuits – and little else – because the strain of the years of saving has given us both chronic stomach trouble.'

We also have an obsession, or we believe we have, with not messing our food about. And yet this is manifestly illogical. All our famous dishes are messed about in some way: Lancashire hotpot, black pudding, brawn, sausages, game pie, steak and kidney pie, Cornish pasties, veal and ham pie. But we like to put about this image of ourselves as preferring simple honest food like roast beef when, in fact, we like our food as mucked about as anyone else. A very common fallacy was expressed some time ago in a letter to the *Daily Mail*:

'The reason the French mess everything about in casseroles and such-like dishes, is they cannot procure the quality of meat obtainable in Britain; and they wouldn't know how to cook it anyway.'

On analysis, this deep prejudice against mucked-about food becomes absurd. No food is more 'mucked about', if that phrase means 'elaborately prepared', than Chinese and Indian food, and yet there has been a phenomenal rise in the number of Oriental restaurants in Britain. A Unilever market research report established that six times as many people in Britain have eaten in a Chinese restaurant as in, say, an Italian restaurant. So it can't be mucked about food we don't like. And yet, the prejudice is deep rooted. 'You don't fancy it' is a common attitude to eating abroad. Hence the great quantity of emergency rations taken abroad by British campers. A letter in the *Glasgow Evening Times* revealed that even in the 1960's, our national suspicions die hard:

'Butchers tell us that if we join the Common Market, there may be delays in delivery to us. Surely this does not mean that we will have to send our good Scotch meat to a central market and, in return, take delivery of Continental horsemeat, frogs' legs, or anything so disgusting.'

Even when it comes to bread, we prefer our own chalk-white steam-baked product to that fresh crusty stuff they sell in France. If you don't believe me, read this letter from the *Leicester Mercury*:

'We went to France for our holidays and took six large sliced loaves of bread with us. We still had one left after thirteen days. It was still good to eat. This is a tribute to a Leicester bakery.'

It's a very wonderful tribute, too, to the resilience of the British palate.

We like what we like

'The bulk of the population of these islands is quite
insensitive and unimaginative. At mealtimes they are
quite satisfied with overcooked meat and overboiled potatoes,
with salad creams, bottled mayonnaise and other concoctions
abominable to gourmets'

André Simon, writing in The Times, *January* 1957

'As for fresh fruit, it is taboo. Not once in five months have
we been offered an orange, apple or pear. Twice only have
we had fresh grapefruit to begin breakfast, but it was small
and bitter'

Innocents in Britain *by Willard Price, published* 1958

Not long ago I asked a hotelier why he thought the majority of people in Britain were prepared to put up with badly cooked food. His theory was that as a nation we're still not used to eating out. Although a few older people, who have had the privilege of travelling in Europe know what good food should taste like, the younger generation are not sure. They take their indecision into restaurants with them and they lack the confidence to complain even if they feel instinctively that what they are eating is badly cooked. With wine they are even more at a loss. The result is that the average restaurateur can, and frequently does, get away with practices that his counterpart in France, Belgium or Italy couldn't. In passing we should note that if the customer is ignorant of wine-lore, he's often in good company. A catering journalist reported recently: 'In an expensive restaurant (which had better be nameless) a friend of mine asked what vintage ports they had. One was brought which the waiter assured us was 40 years old. Pressed to identify it he vanished to return with the information: "It is from Portugal, sir." Another waitress when asked what sort of wine was in the carafe said: "I don't know exactly but it is made from grapes!"'
A Hampshire caterer told me: 'By and large the easiest customers in the world are the British. Breaking it down to regions, the easiest people I know to satisfy are people from industrial areas. You can give them rubbish and they will eat it, and pay for it, and thank you. The hardest people to satisfy are country people and Londoners.'
A woman who's had a great deal of experience in the field is Joy Barnett of the Food Education Society. When I asked her why our standards were so low, she put it like this:

'You can't expect a country which has no tradition of anything except the treatment of its own indigenous foods which are now no longer available to any but the very, very few, to have any notion of how to behave when faced with the bewildering variety of foods you get today. The housewife

is being offered "convenience" foods all the time, but she
hasn't any tradition about how and when to use them to her
advantage. This lack of knowledge of food handling runs
right through everything. That is why quite a lot of
middle-class catering today is failing horribly because it's
trying to give people roast lamb and mint sauce for an
uneconomic price, whereas if they had the traditions of the
French and Belgians, they could make cheap meat into heavenly
appetising dishes with, let's face it, some skill in
handling but not to an extent that it would be impossible to
learn. The average British caterer, and I mean by this Fred's
Café, has got a man who can fry bacon and eggs, serve a
cup of tea and a couple of bits of bread. I would rather have
decent bacon and eggs than one of those ghastly pretentious
meals in a ghastly pretentious little restaurant which tarts
everything up with a bad sauce – at least Fred's bacon and
eggs is honest and even Fred finds difficulty in spoiling bacon
and egg!'

It seems that bacon and egg isn't enough, though. We want
elaborate, pretentious food as well. Joy Barnett is convinced,
as she put it, that,

'the social connotations of eating are far more important than
any question of palate among the masses. People say they
like pâté and melon because they equate this with what
they've seen on the screen, and it's a bit more up the market
than soup – a bit posher. Of course, the universal practice of
serving "pre-mixes" which make the soup taste like library
paste flavoured with tomato or mulligatawny may have
hastened the process!'

There is a certain amount of despair in the industry about the
taste of the average customer. As a chef said when he was
analysing for me the undemanding nature of the
British:

'It all begins in the home – you look in any butcher's shop on

Friday or Saturday. There are all the little joints of beef all done up with string and just enough for four, with a bit left over for mincing on Monday. It's all topside! Now, any decent butcher would tell you that the last thing you want to do with topside is put it in a hot oven and bake it until it's as dry as leather. But that's the Sunday ritual pattern in Britain. The average British housewife is a lazy slut, she doesn't know what's it's all about and she doesn't care.'

Exaggerated? I wonder. I was told of the suburban housewife who went into her greengrocer's. The following conversation took place:

SHE *looking round miserably* You haven't got anything really much today, have you?

HE Madam, I've got carrots, parsnips, turnips, beetroots, sprouts, lettuce, tomatoes, cabbage, celery, brussel sprouts, artichokes, celeriac, swedes . . .

SHE *dejectedly* Oh well, then I'd better have some frozen peas.

Nothing he had was really worth the bother of cutting or peeling or slicing. If you happen to be a housewife and you're not like that, then your husband's very lucky. But next time you're passing a television set, watch the commercials. They seem mostly to be addressed to women whose only kitchen tools are a pair of scissors for cutting polythene and foil wrappings, and a tin opener. A great deal of research and creative energy goes into these commercials, and they're not there for laughs. This pretty woman in the afternoon frock, with her hair freshly done and looking ready to leap into bed with the first man to come through the door, is Mrs Average Housewife, or how the advertising men suggest the manufacturer should see Mrs A.H. She is far too busy compulsively forcing grey out and forcing white in to her husband's shirts to spend more than a few minutes a day at the

cooker. For her, everything must be EASY. As she is largely illiterate, gaining most of her information from the screen, she doesn't want lots of instructions. What she likes to do is un-zip the foil envelope, place contents in pan of water and stir over a low flame for 2 minutes. Or she likes to empty a packet into a bowl, add an egg, whisk, and there you have it ready to pop in the oven. Or she likes to drop a cube into the leftovers of that old Sunday joint and produce something that will make hubby desire her very much. Or she likes to open tins full of rich fresh goodness (just add half a pint of milk) or little containers of chemicals that will, theoretically, make featherlight pancakes or heavenly buns or whatever it says on the packet.

For Mrs A.H., as portrayed in TV commercials, the less time spent in the kitchen the better. Nobody has yet done a survey on what the children of Mrs A.H. have for supper, but I wouldn't mind betting that in 98% of homes it's some kind of quick convenience food: baked beans, frozen hamburgers, spaghetti with tomato sauce, tinned soup, fish fingers, tinned meat loaf. It's small wonder that a population that has been brought up almost entirely on processed food should not be over-demanding when it eats out.

I had some documentary evidence about the unambitious nature of the food in one middle-class household from a University student:

'Have been lodging with the L's for one term now but hope to move at Christmas. No seeming shortage of money; three kids well-dressed; Triumph 2000 in drive; husband managerial. Diet interesting: children live on sweets, biscuits, ice-cream, mineral waters, coke, fish fingers, Chipples, cake, slices of bread and tins of luncheon meat. Our diet almost the the same. So far only fresh vegetable bought by Mrs L. has been lettuce which she can't get frozen. Our staple is tinned cream of tomato soup, frozen peas and pies made with tinned fruits. Husband very fond of chocolate sponge pudding and synthetic cream. Meat, once a week. Joint of some nameless part of cow, usually badly cooked and tough. Used up later in week minced etc. From discussion with fellow students my diet not at all unusual for area. I sneak out and buy apples and pears and eat them surreptitiously in my room like smuggled contraband.'

What food tastes like is not very important. It is still common practice in many British households for a mid-day meal to be put aside on a plate, allowed to cool in the oven and then re-heated as a supper for the man of the house. If you've ever had a meal cooked at midday, allowed to cool until six in the evening and then steamed for an hour over a saucepan of water, you'll realize the full extent of our contribution to the field of international cuisine.
Very little research has been done on what we could call our 'food ways'. But some astonishing facts have been collected about national eating habits by the Market Research Division of W. S. Crawford Ltd. It seems we're not very experimental with our food. Winter and summer, the ritual Sunday lunch in the majority of British homes remains either roast beef or roast lamb. Top of the pudding popularity poll is custard accompanied by milk pudding or some kind of stewed fruit. Custard is eaten by more people than any other single form of dessert. It may strike the foreign observer as indomitable masochism that makes us cover our 'afters' so thickly and often with a bilious, yellow goo composed, as one custard powder packet stated quite openly, of 'edible starch, salt, flavouring and colouring'.
During the week the majority of men (six out of ten) go home to a midday meal and the food varies very little between a cold winter day and a hot summer day. Another survey, carried out by the Industrial Welfare Society, has revealed that throughout the year, whatever the weather, the top ten dishes in the British works canteen remain roughly the same. They are – in descending order of popularity – roast

beef, steak and kidney pie, fish and chips, liver and bacon, ham and chips, steak pudding, savoury mince, stewed steak, hot pot, and bottom of the list, (not surprising when you consider the quality of most of them,) sausages. The three top sweets are: apple pie, rice pudding and steamed jam roll. Butlin's, the great holiday-camp pioneers, reflect these tastes in their daily holiday menus. A random Sunday lunch at Clacton in 1966 consisted of Romany soup made from a packet, roast beef, roast and boiled potatoes, carrots and cabbage, followed by tinned peaches and cream.

When you enquire into the figures you find that, on any given evening, only a small proportion of the population are eating anywhere other than in the comfort of their own homes. In the days when television used to indulge in late-night programmes where the guests chatted over brandy and cigars after dinner, the majority of viewers must have found their behaviour almost perversely eccentric. To be discovered still at 'dinner' at nine thirty in the evening is like being found having breakfast at three in the afternoon. Research has revealed that by 7 p.m. 74% of Britain is already half way through its evening meal. Only one in twenty would dream of eating a large evening meal after eight o'clock at night. This, of course, accounts for the very sharp looks you're thrown in the more conventional hotel if you amble into dinner much after half past seven.

Foreigners fortunate enough to come across a copy of this book before visiting England should note well the time at which the LARGEST NUMBER of British people eat their meals.

Breakfast	8–8.30
Elevenses	11–11.30
Mid-day meal	1–1.30
Afternoon break	4–4.30
Evening meal	6–6.30

To ask for anything in Britain much outside these hours,

without expecting to pay heavily for it, is to invite constant disillusion. Visitors from countries as relaxed as Norway must take our little foibles into account. An astonished Englishman from Exeter, staying at a Norwegian hotel last summer, was delighted to find breakfast served from 7.30–11, lunch from 12.30–6 and dinner from 7–11!

As a nation we tend not to eat out if we can help it. Perhaps wisely so. The average worker spends just over £16 a year in his canteen but, apart from his annual holiday and the odd celebration supper, eating out plays a minor part in his life. The Crawford survey revealed that on an average week-day night in the winter only 2% of people interviewed ate out. Even on Saturday, which is the night when we British traditionally live it up, the figure was the same. In summer, however, you may find as many as five people in a hundred actually venturing out in the evening to chance their arm in a café, restaurant or hotel. In fairness, one ought to point out that the summer figures were obtained in a very hot week in August when a great number of people interviewed were on holiday and therefore doomed to eat out anyway.

Until 1966, no one really knew what people wanted to eat when they went out. But in 1966 the National Catering Inquiry, sponsored by Smethursts Foods Limited, presented its first report – they called it 'The British Eating Out' – and its 34 pages reveal an interesting fact. What the caterer thinks the public wants, and what the public says it wants, don't always tally. For instance, the caterers claimed that the most popular vegetables were peas, brussel sprouts, cabbage and cauliflower, in that order. The customers, however, claimed that *their* favourite vegetables were peas, brussel sprouts, green beans and cauliflower – they rated cabbage *eighth* on their list of preferences.

The same discrepancy between what the caterer thought the customer wanted and what the customer claimed he wanted was apparent in the choice of a main course. The caterers said the customer liked meat, mixed grill and poultry, in that order. The customer said his choice was meat, poultry and only third – mixed grill. In Leeds, for example, 29% of customers said they would choose poultry for a main course, but only 3% of caterers in Leeds thought their customers would do so.

The survey also revealed that a third of Britain only eats out for pleasure 'every few months'. When it does so it prefers a restaurant to a hotel or a café and tends to spend about 13s 2d on a meal – although 51% paid 10s or less, and 29% paid 7s 6d or less.

It appeared that when Mr and Mrs Briton went out for the the night they wanted: good cooking, a clean-looking room, and fast service – in that order. Those were their three top priorities. After that, in descending order, came: hot food, atmosphere, extensive menu, good presentation, friendly service, low prices and large helpings.

It appeared too that the majority slightly preferred waiters to waitresses, background music to silence, and they disliked a service charge. In the light of these preferences it is interesting to note that in Britain there are two waitresses for every waiter, only 34% of caterers provide background music, and the service charge is becoming standard practice.

As an outside observer I find it difficult to connect what the British public *says* it wants with what the owner of a small café *knows* it wants. There's no better barometer of mass public taste than the seaside resort. Here the Englishman is on holiday and caterers compete to offer him exactly the meal of his dreams.

The menus are uncannily the same, they vary only minutely from Blackpool to Filey to Clacton, Brighton, Hastings, Paignton, Weston-super-Mare and Llandudno. There may be slight regional preferences but the overall uniformity is startling. Here, for instance, is a menu, an archetypal one, from a café in Hornsea, a small seaside town on the east coast of Yorkshire; the date Good Friday, 1966:

SET LUNCH

Soup or fruit juice, roast beef, 2 veg.
fruit pie, custard and cup of tea 6/-
(children 3/6)

or

Bacon egg and tomatoes	4/-
Baked beans and chips	2/6
Fried egg and chips	3/-
Ham egg and chips	5/6
Sausage and chips	4/-
Chicken and chips	5/-
Hamburger and chips	4/-
Poached egg on toast	2/9
Steak and kidney pie chips and peas	3/6
Cod and chips	3/6
Haddock and chips	4/-
Halibut and chips	5/6
Plaice and chips	5/-

(all dishes include, tea, bread and
butter)

Basically this sort of menu hasn't changed for 30 or 40 years, perhaps longer; the only post-war novelty is the hamburger. When I'm told by food writers that a revolution is sweeping across the country and that it's all scampi now, and pâté and melon, I take out my file of seaside café menus to reassure myself that in the rainswept frontline of Britain, its still chips yesterday, chips today and chips tomorrow – and fruit pie and custard to follow please.

A certain lack of dignity

'Overall there is a lack of dignity in British catering. It's a national problem. Catering is personal service of one human being to another and, if it's not done with dignity, it's not done well.'

A restaurant manager

'Although there are pockets of enlightenment, the general picture is one of dismal confusion, of an unwillingness to train when the labour turnover is so high and a refusal to acknowledge the Victorian conditions under which many waiters work.'

Desmond Ryan writing in The Hotel and Catering Review, *January* 1966

'There's a helluva lot of cowboys in catering, because they don't fit in anywhere else. Our veg. cook is one of them – I couldn't see him doing anything else except perhaps sweeping the roads.'

A Chef

'I am convinced most of the pilfering and sharp practice which occurs with staff is largely due to the bad living-conditions and low wages which are being paid by large hotels . . . I would like to see some photographs of staff living quarters appear in national newspapers. Some of the managements would have exceedingly red faces.'

Extract from letter in The Caterer and Hotel-keeper, *March* 17*th*, 1966

Those four quotations are symptomatic of a wide-spread malaise in the catering business today. It is why more and more workers are leaving hotels and restaurants and moving into industrial catering where they feel they can retain their dignity and self-respect. A letter which was published in a catering journal at the beginning of 1966 focused attention not only on the unhappiness that exists in certain sections of the industry, but on one of the reasons behind the chronic shortage of labour:

'My New Year resolution may interest you because I believe it has also been made by a number of my friends in the catering trade. It is never to accept another post in a hotel. After 25 years (eleven as *chef de cuisine*), I am now only interested in industrial catering.

. . . I both love and take pride in my work. When I married, I even taught my wife to be a *pâtissier* so that we could work together.

I have worked in five-star hotels with a full brigade down to a single-handed position . . . Unfortunately the whole concept of catering has changed in the past ten years. In hotels this change has been for the worse . . .

I have finally excommunicated myself. My new employer does not profess to know my job better than I do. He tells me what he wants, and leaves me to do the job I was trained to do and that he pays me to do. I have the most modern equipment and a spacious kitchen. I have a happy staff who haven't to try to do two days work in one. Most important of all, I respect my employer . . .'

The dissatisfaction revealed in this letter was reflected in a talk I had with Michael Nightingale of the Hotel and Catering Institute. He pointed out that industrial firms had a long tradition of treating their staff well and operating in a rational industrial way. 'They have personnel officers, they use proper management techniques. This has spread over to the catering departments, and caterers, who have gone into these companies, have been suddenly involved in this atmosphere and therefore they have improved. Now, in hotels and restaurants they've not had this direct industrial influence and, in fact, hoteliers and restaurateurs think they are different from any other industry. They even think they are different from industrial caterers, although it's often the same man with the same training doing the same job.'

Many workers on the non-industrial side of catering are convinced that they are being imposed upon, or not appreciated, or taken advantage of in some way. To the student fresh from college, the descent into the kitchens of a big hotel sometimes comes as a shock when he finds that the general acceptance of the short-cut and the second best is all too common. Two years out of college, one ex-student told me, 'At college you're taught to do all these things properly, but where I'm working most of the things aren't done as well as I've been taught. You know, like putting vinegar into the mayonnaise and sending it out as hollandaise, or serving the left-over coffee from lunch to people having dinner, and everything frozen because there's more profit in frozen than fresh.'

There is such an element of farce in some restaurants that very little dignity can remain for those who have to work there. A lot of the farce seems to be demanded by the customers. For instance, the passion for having raging bonfires beside the table would be enough to disenchant any self-respecting waiter. I did once hear a couple ask if the *coq au vin* could be cooked at the table as seeing it done was such fun. I'm sure that before long I'm going to go into a really pretentious place and find them preparing luncheon meat *flambé*, with great sheets of flame and squeals of excitement from the guests – after all, as we shall see later in this book, eating out is supposed to be a dramatic experience – and such a performance would no doubt qualify, if only as third-rate *opera bouffe*.

How much of the unhappiness in the catering business can be

attributed to the customers and how much to the working conditions is a matter for argument. But let's for a moment look at the part *we* play in creating the sort of service which we eventually receive. Many waiters I've talked to have made no attempt to conceal their contempt for the lack of knowledge of the British about food. 'When it comes to food, they stick to one or two dishes they know,' one waiter told me. 'And when it comes to wine they usually pick the second cheapest one on the menu, and usually it's quite unsuitable for the food they've ordered – most of them disgust me. They only deserve cold fish and chips!'

For perhaps a more reasoned explanation of why standards are so low in this country I include this verbatim diatribe from a man who still runs a very good restaurant:

'When I began I was determined not to compromise on anything. You know, the best butter, the best meat, the best fish, the best vegetables, the best fruit. I brought over a first-class chef, and I had really good Italian boys waiting at table. That was ten years ago. You've had lunch here today and you know what standards we maintain but really I often wonder why. Perhaps once in a blue moon someone comes here who really understands what we're doing. The rest of the time I could throw rock salmon, chips and tinned peas on the table and charge a fiver for it. They're like a lot of arrogant sheep. They don't come to enjoy a civilized meal, they come to stuff themselves and see how much they can spend. If I put asparagus on the menus at thirty five bob a stick, some fool, showing off to a client, would buy it. They really *like* tinned food. They don't care if the meat is falling off the bone from over-cooking. You could pour vinegar in the glass as long as you told them it was chateau bottled! And yet one keeps smiling. The stories I could tell you, you wouldn't believe it.'

Some of the stories he told me appear elsewhere in this book. One or two nobody could print and get away with. Well, let

me try one. The man, for instance, whose bill came to £2 5s.
On the plate he left a cheque for £25. Three days later a
letter of complaint arrived. He would willingly have paid £10
he said, but felt £25 was 'gross profiteering'. I asked this
restaurateur if he could describe a typical 'bad customer'. Had
I noticed, he asked a well-dressed couple sitting in the corner of
the restaurant. They had arrived at one o'clock in a chauffeur
driven Bentley. I said I had. 'Well now, they're a very special
cross I bear. He made, or so the story goes, just over a quarter
of a million by inventing ———. He sold his company
and he now gets a very handsome salary as a director of the
firm he sold out to. They came down here last year, bought
themselves a large house, and I suppose they're semi-retired.
They have a flat in Spain where they go every summer, and
they usually take a P. & O cruise in the winter. His hobby is

carpentry, but how she passes the time I can't think. They come here at one every week-day and there's a sort of ritual. He always starts with soup, whatever it is – if I put rat soup on the menu he'd order it. He has half a bottle of Blue Nun Liebfraumilch whatever he's eating, and she has a port to start with and then half a bottle of some kind of Sauternes. She rings the changes on those, but her wine has to be nice and sweet. He has boiled potatoes with every lunch and either peas or carrots or, when it's in season, asparagus which he's very partial to. She picks her way about among the expensive dishes but usually has Steak Diane because she likes the drama and attention at the table. They don't usually have anything after that, but he has a cigar and brandy with his coffee, and she has a *crème de menthe frappé*. I suppose they spend an average of twenty pounds or so a week here and, if they bring friends for dinner on Saturday night, it's more. Any discrimination, sense of taste, or feeling for food is completely lacking, and I despise myself for taking their money.'

If we are ignorant about food, we are also very self-conscious about it. There's a built-in fear among us of making a scene or attracting the wrong sort of attention.

The average diner-out will usually steer clear of anything elaborate or unnecessarily expensive, unless he is thoroughly conditioned to it. Today most people will eat scampi; in fact, if you were to consult hotel menus you might assume that they won't eat anything else. Those who have been to Spain will expose themselves on occasion to *paella*, but by and large, our tastes remain inelastic. In 1947, for instance, the Gallup Poll asked a representative cross-section of Britons this question 'If expense were no object and you could have absolutely anything you wanted, what would you choose for a perfect meal?' The answer was: tomato soup, sole, roast chicken, roast potatoes, peas and sprouts, trifle and cream, and cheese and biscuits. In 1962 a similar survey was undertaken and revealed that 15 years later the Briton's perfect meal was exactly the same, except that he would now prefer fruit salad to trifle. The more we venture out of the rut, the more likely we are to be disappointed and so our motto remains 'play it safe'. If something were to go wrong, like finding a human toe in the soup, the best thing to do would be to call quietly for the bill and leave. Complaining on the spot is almost invariably resented, and complaining afterwards often brings only delayed rudeness. On one occasion some friends of mine had a very bad meal in a restaurant but, in the best British tradition, paid up and left quietly. The woman brooded on this meal so much that eventually, to exorcise herself, she wrote to the manager and said that although they had given a tip, they really felt they had received no service whatsoever. A few days later a curt note arrived with a postal order for 8s, the amount they had left on the plate.

I know of only one authenticated case of a diner being physically assaulted after registering a complaint, but appeals to the management may often leave you with the feeling that you are overdemanding, uncouth, ill-mannered, socially inadequate and wrong. The management's contention that nobody, in a right and proper state of mind, does complain is borne out by the almost invariable reply to any complaint: 'I'm most awfully sorry this has happened sir. I can assure you *it's the first complaint we've had!*' or 'Of course we'll change it, sir, but *all our other customers have found it very enjoyable.*' By the patient, idiot-humouring tone of voice, you and the other diners within a twelve table radius are reminded that the fault, if fault there is, certainly doesn't lie with the management.

I once observed a duel of this kind between a restaurant manager and a customer:

'*Yes sir, I understand you're not happy about your ham?*'
'Well, I don't like complaining but really it is 11s 6d a plate.

I mean look at it!'

'*Yes sir – what precisely were you objecting to?*'

'Well, what there is, is mostly fat. I particularly asked for a lean portion.'

'*I'm most sorry about that, sir, but you must appreciate that this isn't TINNED ham. It's the very finest York ham cooked here in our own kitchens, and it's cut fresh off the bone. You'll appreciate that we can't give you all the lean (raising his voice) and leave the fat for everyone else. I mean, that's not the way a restaurant is run, not this restaurant anyway.*'

'I certainly don't want ALL the lean. I just wanted a reasonable amount – to go with the fat.'

'*Yes I understand, sir, I must say we've been serving our York hams in this restaurant for seventeen years, and this is the first complaint we've had. But if you are on a special diet, I'll see what can be done.*'

The owner left triumphantly, nodding and smiling to his other guests. A few minutes later a waiter returned with a fresh plate overpiled with a great Everest of ham. The point had been dramatically made!

Because the British in their daily social life cultivate a façade of politeness – a convention which enables two people who regard each other with total hostility to chat happily together in public – they regard it as logical to carry this façade of politeness into hotels and restaurants.

An Englishman would rather submit to voluntary euthanasia than expose himself to the possibility of Raised Voices in Public. To be revealed in a naked argument with some wretched foreign waiter over a bowl of soup would be as unthinkable as walking down Threadneedle Street in Bermuda shorts. To be found quarrelling with a fellow Englishman, even though he was temporarily disguised in a waiter's outfit, would be socially even more shaming. I have a feeling that this reticence is traded on. The average waiter, or waitress, knows that you are aware that waiting is, in itself, a menial and ignoble function, and he or she relies on your decency not to make it even more intolerable by complaining about a wrongly added-up bill or stale food. And even if you do complain, you won't get very far. We also possess a sense of fair play, summed up in phrases like 'well, she's doing her best' or 'she must be rushed off her feet' or 'poor soul, I'm glad it's not me'. Many English waiters presume upon an easy familiarity with their customers that is not often discouraged. 'Right friends, what's your poison' provoked a chuckle in the dining-car on a journey I made to Edinburgh. Mind you that particular waiter was a bit of a card; he announced his lightning dashes up and down the corridor with the old naval cry, 'Make way for an officer and a gentleman!' There was the waitress in a hotel in Kent whom I heard calling a Bishop 'darling'. She flushed him out from behind the *Daily Telegraph* with the words, 'Come on, darling. You've been sitting over that pot of tea quite long enough, the bar's been open half an hour!' Sometimes these familiarities are resented. 'This England' recorded recently the letter in the *Sunday Times* which ran, ' "Do you gents want something to drink?" though said in a perfectly friendly manner was not, in my view, the right way for a wine waiter to address First Class passengers'. But we don't usually mind about waiters. I recall the sympathetic audience of diners in the small Kentish hotel who, on a summer's evening, were being waited on by a white-haired old man who was not only all alone, but also incredibly plastered. His performance with the very full plates of powdered tomato soup had the split-second timing of a Tati. Halfway through the meal, he leered, bade us all goodnight, and backed out of the room bowing. We found out afterwards from the very cross manageress that he had 'had one of his turns and had gone to lie down.'

And there was the tipsy waiter at the steak house who, when I ordered a glass of red wine, insisted on pouring half a glass for me to try. When I told him that I'd had it before and it was pretty horrid and there was no reason to think that if I tried it it would get any better, he said, 'Ah, but if you

33

try it, then I can fill your glass again and you get more that
way.'

It's the sort of mateyness that often dissolves anger and induces
a mild attack of deflation. That the service is often amateur,
sometimes offensive, seldom perfect, does not seem to distress
us unduly. As a nation we have an inexhaustible fund of
patience. Perhaps we are, after all, a kindly people. Or is it,
as a waiter put it, more like this. 'You couldn't get away with
it anywhere else, but honestly they'll put up with bloody
murder in this country and if you give 'em the old bow and
scrape bit, they're almost falling over themselves to press a
tip into your hand . . . who'd be a waiter?'

Are the scampi fresh, Bruno?

'Jelly & Evap. Milk. is'

From an Oxford café menu

'L'Oeuf sur le Plat Bercy (Egg with grilled sausage, tomato sauce)'

Item from menu outside Wimbledon hotel

'Le melon refraîchi à son apogée . . . The season's finest melon, dawn-chilled'

Item from West End restaurant menu

There are two kinds of bad food in Britain: bad cheap food
and bad expensive food. There's more bad cheap food about,
so let's look at that first. Bad cheap food is not normally
brought to the notice of well-off people. That's probably why
railway refreshment rooms are singled out for such
disparagement in the correspondence columns of *The Times*.
If you are a member of the small élite who have been used to
eating reasonably good food in gracious surroundings,
entering the cup of tea and pork pie world of the railway
platform could send you into a mild state of shock followed
by compulsive letter writing. Upper crust people assume, all
too wrongly, that the urns and buns and cheese rolls are an
invention of British Rail. What they are in fact seeing is one
facet of the nether-world of the working-class café, where
indifferent food can be eaten cheaply and quickly. A
similar sense of outrage overtook a team of journalists
who, in 1964, prepared a survey of cheap food in *The People*.
They decided that there were plenty of guides for those who
had money to burn but:

'What about the holiday folk who simply want to know where
to get a good honest meal cleanly served and at a fair price?'

They set off round the popular resorts of Britain where the
'holiday folk' go. They found a tidal wave of filth and bad
food nearly everywhere. The picture they drew was one of
squalor relieved only occasionally by some caterer giving
value for money in clean surroundings.
In Margate they ate in a restaurant seating 200 which
resembled a works canteen. 'It was nearly 20 minutes before
our order was taken, but after that the service was reasonably
fast. The roast beef was nothing to write home about but
the sweet – apple pie and custard, 1s 3d – was far larger than
we received anywhere else in Margate. But, sadly, we noted
the other things – the old stains still showing on the plastic
table-top, the chipped crockery, water stains on the knives
and forks from where they had been rinsed but not dried.

When the plump, harassed waitress eventually brought our tea, we found one of the cups marked and grimed with dirt and tea stains.'

On to Blackpool where very few restaurants fulfilled the criteria 'good plain food served in generous portions in clean surroundings at a reasonable price'. They described one of the cheapest places to eat like this: 'The floor was dirty, the plates chipped, the tables tiny, the salt and pepper pots greasy. The soup and custard were lumpy – usually the result of being kept around too long. The main course food was tasteless.'

My guess was that the soup and custard were lumpy not only because they were kept around too long, but because they were inexpertly made, as most soup and custard is these days, from powder.

The team of experts went to a plush modern restaurant advertising 'Olde English Fare'. 'We ordered a 4s hamburger which turned out to be red-raw, swimming in grease and accompanied by cold, soggy chips and an unappetizing mess of oily fried onions.' At Southsea there were more gastronomic disappointments: in one restaurant they reported 'unfriendly service, chipped crockery, un-emptied ashtrays and sugar bottles open to flies and dirt. We tried steak and chips at 5s 6d and found it unappetizing. The steak was still attached to pieces of the plastic it had been wrapped in.'

At Morecambe: 'We asked the waitress what soup they were serving, to which she replied rather acidly, "I don't know – I don't work in the kitchen, you know. It could be anything." It turned out to be kidney, complete with dubious lumps, accompanied by a quarter slice of dry bread. The only 4s 6d lunches were steak and kidney pie or steak pudding. We opted for the pie, and got half of one of those pies you can buy anywhere for 10d, cut diagonally and doused with gravy.'

The team did find places where they got value for money, but their conclusion was damning: 'Brighton is the only resort we have come across so far where the good restaurants outnumber the bad.'

I, too, have had depressing meals in cafés like the ones described in *The People* report. The memory is of custard, hard grey pastry, thick processed soups with a predominant colour of red lead, wafer-thin slices of warmed-up meat, limp chips, tinned vegetables, cups of horrible coffee (made with milk and coffee powder) all served in surroundings aggressively void of charm or comfort. This is the sort of food the average Briton eats when he goes out, and these are the kind of conditions he eats it in. This is the standard of catering which has earned for Britain what John Fuller, Director of the Scottish Hotel School, described at a seminar in Spring 1966, as 'a rather sinister reputation by international standards'.

What about bad *expensive* food? It flourishes mainly in towns where businessmen gratify each other with smoked salmon and mixed grills and quivering ice-cream sundaes. It flourishes in the country, too, where an inn serves ostentatious food with a flourish to the Jaguar-driving farmers and their potted-shrimp-eating wives. This is the world of taped background music, frozen vegetables, tasteless but tender steaks, Chicken Maryland and *crêpes suzettes* flaring at the table. Here are some notes made in 1965 and 1966 while on safari in middle-class Britain.

CASE ONE Small country inn, Home Counties. Clientele at lunchtime, groups of executives from nearby manufacturing town. Man called Roland snaps his fingers for head-waiter whom he introduces to his three guests with the words, 'This is Bruno, the best head-waiter in Britain.' Bruno smiles diffidently, knowing he isn't. 'Now Bruno, are the scampi fresh? Yes or no! Because these gentlemen have come all the way from Sweden, and they know all about fish in Sweden.' Bruno smiles and tells them that the scampi are always fresh. They order scampi all round and 'some of your really tender steaks, Bruno, nicely done – wonderful meat here you know!' The menu, when we flush Bruno out from his high-tipping businessmen, is the standard plastic-coated card which I always feel is mass-printed in some central headquarters, and handed out like hymn sheets to what a friend of mine has named 'the scampi restaurants'. To start, there is smoked salmon, avocado pear (*vinaigrette* or with prawns), smoked trout, potted shrimps, *pâté maison* (from a tin), seafood cocktail, tinned snails, melon and Parma ham, *minestrone*, *consommé* with sherry, and asparagus soup. I always get a sinking feeling when I see that well-tried muster roll of convenience foods. The taste is always the same, only the price varies – and that is dependent on just how much the clients will pay without rioting. For a main course, we have the ubiquitous steak which will be garnished, I don't know why, with parsley butter, and its old stable companions the mixed grill, Chicken Maryland, roast duckling, sole *meunière*, whitebait, *coq au vin*, Lobster Thermidor, kebabs in a bed of instant de-flavoured rice and grilled gammon steak. To wedge all that lot in there's the cheeseboard, 'dairy' ices, chocolate *mousse*, 'homemade' apple pie, and *ananas au kirsch*, which is a great favourite with the businessmen because Bruno is quite lavish with the kirsch. Having seen the menu, we drink up our Managing Director's Keg Special served in a pewter tankard and leave, catching a last glimpse of Bruno warming great balloon glasses over a naked flame for a party of export drivers, red-faced and sweating from their labours at the trough – 'Bruno always warms the glass you know – brings out the bouquet! Cigars everyone?'

CASE TWO   Two friends flying off to Bangkok just before Christmas turned up with one day to spare. We drove them, having carefully booked a table, to a delightful part of Surrey. We were going, we said, to a small inn where we had lunched once before. The food was good and it specialized in a huge variety of well-prepared *fresh* vegetables. FRESH, we told them, none of your chemically treated, tinned, tasteless trash, but fresh out of the garden. Perhaps we were a little put off when, on the way, we came to read the entry in the *Good Food Guide*, 'Since a partial change of management a year ago, raptures have moderated somewhat . . .' 'Some folk are too hypercritical' we told ourselves and drove on, anticipation high. The broth was good, our spirits rose – this was going to be a memorable meal. The duckling arrived, braised in Curaçao, then the vegetables. Carrots, peas and corn on the cob. Carrots tinned, obviously, with that shorn plastic look that all good tinned carrots have. The maize – well, tinned or frozen, it was tasteless. The peas – frozen, probably, tinned possibly, the palate by that time had lost interest. The duck (at £2 10s for the four of us) was overdone and falling off the bone. The Stilton which followed was dried out. The waitress apologized for its decayed state and drew our attention to a handsome prime slice of Cheddar. But, if the Stilton was finished, why wasn't it pensioned off and a new one procured? After all, at 2s 6d a portion, the profit margin would have allowed the chef to invest in a presentable Stilton . . . still, if we'd been a few weeks early, we might have been luckier.

To redeem the meal we thought we might have a drink with our coffee. It was 2.35 p.m. No drinks, said the waitress. The bar closed five minutes ago and the barman has gone home. 'Could you not,' we said, 'have warned us that the bar was about to close as they do in other places which have early closing hours.' 'We don't tell people,' she said. 'I think you should tell people in future,' I said, and she looked offended. I wrote a letter of complaint to the inn and also asked them why it was economically impossible, at the high prices they were charging, to serve fresh vegetables in season. My letter pointed out that the current copy of the *Hotel and Catering Times* revealed that fresh cabbage, carrots, cauliflowers, mushrooms, onions, parsnips, turnips and sprouts were all in cheap and plentiful supply. I got this reply: 'Receipt of your letter dated 14th December, 1965 is acknowledged and is receiving our attention. A reply will be forwarded to you in due course.' It still hasn't arrived.

CASE THREE A meal which we had in a delightful Georgian coaching inn, 'somewhere in Wessex', is perhaps typical of how very often what should be a pleasant occasion is turned into a numbing agony.

The food, once you contrived to get it, was the usual 11s 6d chain hotel lunch. The dining room was presided over by a headwaiter in his early seventies in flapping tails, and everything had got totally out of his hands long before we arrived. There were fifteen tables with about 45 to 50 people. To serve them was the old man who, in fact, was permanently *hors de combat* wrestling with bottles of light ale which seemed to erupt all over everything by the time he'd finished shaking them up. There was a village lad and a village lass, red in the face with confusion, and the situation was only saved by an imperturbable body from Inverness who had the whole room to run. We waited twenty minutes, which is a long time with two hungry children twisting in their seats to watch other people eat. The order had been taken within the first five minutes by the old man who had then stuck it on a spike on his sideboard. We found out later that as he always muddled the orders, to avoid confusion nobody took any notice of them. After twenty minutes, the Scots body arrived with a flurry, removed dishes, flicked crumbs, fetched paper napkins, (carefully cut in half to remind us of wartime shortages) and took the order quickly, kindly and comfortingly. Ten minutes later the packet soup came and, after a fairly lengthy interval for digestion, up steamed our waitress: 'There's the curry for the wee girlie. The steak pie was off, so I've brought you the boiled ham, sir, and the veg will be here directly.' My ten-year-old daughter got a great plate of English-style curry (stewed steak and diced tinned carrots with curry powder added) that would have floored a navvy. I got a child's portion of boiled ham. There was a small problem with the water as they only had one jug in the hotel. ('I've asked them time and time again, but they won't do a thing,' the waitress whispered. 'And the money they're making too!')

We all had tinned fruit salad. The alternative, the 'cheese board', held a crumble of Cheddar. In the hall the manager's wife, in twinset and pearls, hoped we'd had a nice meal: 'We're proud of our name for good food in these parts. Come and visit us again.'

CASE FOUR I was working one day with an American film producer in London and at lunchtime we went to his hotel for something to eat. It was very expensive with lots of good old leather and good old furniture and oil paintings of dead notabilities and defunct game. The head-waiter brought us the menu. My host and his wife, who were domiciled in Athens, Greece, chose steak and green salad. I thought I

43

might have the *Escalope de veau à la Suisse*, not only because I'd never had it, I'd never even heard of it. Perhaps the chef is Swiss, I thought, and this is his big moment. 'Eetsa cookta wiz cheese', explained the head-waiter in that cosmopolitan accent which might conceal somebody from Paris, Rome, Madrid or Potters Bar.

When we got into the restaurant there was a great jug of cold beaded water on the table awash with ice-cubes, a sure sign of a large American clientele. The steaks were brought by two waiters who could have been from Ceylon, India or Pakistan. They spoke no English and were thus not able to communicate when my host asked: 'Which is the rare steak and which is the medium rare?' The correct answer would have been 'Neither!' because, when cut, both steaks turned out to be well done. The portions were gnat-size as was my *escalope* which, on arrival, turned out to be a small piece of fried dark meat (goat?) on which had been grilled a slice of that manufactured cheese which comes pre-sliced in polythene bags and is eminently suitable for making tasteless sandwiches for sale in carmen's pullups. It's what they call a 'convenience cheese'. As I wasn't paying – my *escalope* was 15s 6d – I was denied the pleasure of telling the manager that I thought he was an impudent rogue. My host, who drank white wine reverently with his steak, appeared to find the meal all that might be expected from a first-class London hotel.

CASE FIVE   There was a rather pleasant old inn near London that we used to take the children to for lunch now and again. The kitchen staff were all Italian and so were the waiters. They gave the impression that they enjoyed their job, and they were very good with the children. I suppose we went there eight or nine times over a period of three years. Then one Saturday we arrived, and it was all different. It had been taken over by a very efficient man who had sacked all the Italians. The menu, which had contained some enterprising Continental dishes, was now good solid coaching fare: kidneys and bacon, plaice and chips, gammon steak. The head-waiter charged us for five lunches instead of four and was profuse in his apologies when this was pointed out. Out of curiosity we went again a few months later. There was a great rebuilding on, (imitation Tudor stone fireplaces were being installed,) and this time we were overcharged by 15s 6d. Again the head-waiter was profuse in his apologies. On the way out I met the owner and told him that as I had been overcharged twice running I wasn't coming any more and why didn't he get some waiters who could work out the intricacies of English currency – like all the affable Italians he'd got rid of. Mine host iced up and we parted in silence.

CASE SIX A post-war phenomenon in Britain is the great amount of eating done by families on the verges of busy main roads. Rather than be gyped, thousands of people go to the most elaborate lengths to make themselves self-sufficient. In exhaust-ridden laybys they perch insecurely on canvas chairs while the kettle boils merrily on a primus. The English picnic, one of the most unlovely forms of eating devised, is far preferable to the possible disappointment of bad food, indifferent service and a large bill in some roadside restaurant. On a recent journey north we had no room for the essentials of the picnic (folding tables, teapot, washing-up bowl, transistor stove, to name only half a bootfull) and so one o'clock found us looking out for somewhere to eat. 'Somewhere' turned out to be a rambling stone inn dating back to the advent of the stage-coach. 'If they've been in the catering business that long,' I said as we parked the car, 'this ought to be the place for an honest English lunch.' The restaurant was full but the head-waiter said he would call us when a table was free. We waited in the lounge under a notice saying 'Terms Strictly Cash' while the receptionist and a chambermaid discussed in some detail the reasons why they were both going to give their notice in that Friday. We'd got to the manager's wife who was a 'sneaky

cat' when the head-waiter appeared and led us to a table.
After the traditional pause a waitress arrived with a pencil
and pad: 'Yes, please?' We asked to see the menu and she
had a hunt for one. We examined it as she stood shifting
from foot to foot. It was one of those infuriating (and I
think dishonest) menus which advertises a 12s 6d lunch. On
closer examination it turns out that all the dishes which the
management think will be most popular cost extra. Smoked
salmon was 6s 6d extra, prawn cocktail 5s 6d extra, fried
scampi and sauce tartare 6s extra, whitebait 7s 6d extra. The
main courses were too many and too complicated for an
establishment of that size. Some of them like the steak *garni*
and Surrey capon were also only to be had for a premium. At
the bottom of the menu there were more excess demands –
1s 6d extra for Stilton, 1s 6d for 'dairy cream' and 1s 6d for
coffee. We ordered two eggs mayonnaise and two tomato
soups. The soup was tinned or powdered, the mayonnaise
either bottled or prepared from a pre-mix. The waitress
brought three rolls for the four of us but no butter. She brought
two slices of bread and some butter when asked. After a bit
we asked for water, that was brought too. We had roast
beef, an ample portion but over-cooked, not easy to cut and
tasteless. The children had a peppery stew served with
convenience rice, every grain separate but not much taste.
The vegetables were bruised-looking roast potatoes, scoops of
grey mashed potatoes, tinned carrots and frozen runner beans.
To follow, apart from the extras, were tinned pears, tinned
fruit salad, tinned gooseberries with pastry ('gooseberry tart')'
ice-cream and the cheeseboard – foil-wrapped processed
Gruyère and a hunk of soapy Cheddar. With two glasses of
Beaujolais (Algerian?) at 7s, the bill for the four of us came
to £2 17s. To supplement the wages of the staff (including no
doubt the bickering receptionist and the chambermaid) the
waitress added a gratuitous 10% service charge which I
glumly and uncomplainingly paid as did everyone else in
the room.

What service? Not bringing the butter, or enough rolls,
not bringing water to the table? Carrying two glasses of
wine from the bar (wine grossly overpriced)? Why the ruse
of serving a 12s 6d meal when if one had exercised a choice
it could easily have come to 30s? When we left I read a notice
in the hall which said that there had been an inn on this
site serving food for 450 years. Food like this? The notice
also said that the inn had been a favoured haunt of
highwaymen. 'I reckon they've taken it over,' said my wife
as we got in the car.

CASE SEVEN 'If you're writing a book about food, you ought
to go to the Jolly Fiddlers at Puddingly . . .' That was what
the letter said, and it went on to say that we'd have to
to book several weeks in advance and the meal had to be
ordered the day before by 'phone or in writing and that
M. Yves Crapoule, half-Parisian, half-Liverpudlian, who
owned the place, might refuse you admission if he didn't
take a shine to you. Women were not allowed to wear scent
and smoking was prohibited on the premises. The letter
described M. Crapoule as a cross between General Martinet
and Cynrano de Bergerac, and said that Mme Crapoule did
the cooking and a large army of relatives waited at table.
We booked for three months ahead and the day before rang
again to order the food. What could we have?

'Madame has the whole of *haute cuisine* at her fingertips.'
'Well, in that case we'd like something simple. What about
Veal Marsala?'
'We don't do that.'
'Well, supposing we start with . . .'
'You will begin with *potage purée de gibier* and then you will
have *tournedos Bordelaise* and *crêpes Puddingly* to follow. And
one more thing . . .'
'Yes?'
'Don't be late!'

47

We got to Puddingly on a very wet windy day in September. As the inn was some distance from London we had arranged to stay the night. The Jolly Fiddlers was shut and barred at four in the afternoon and all we got from banging on the door was raw knuckles. We looked in the church where the passage of the centuries had been effectively obliterated by restoration in the 1850's, had a quick tour of the graveyard and wound up with another banging session on all four visible doors of the Fiddlers. After that we drove round and round the flat, damp countryside, which was as empty as if hurriedly evacuated after some natural disaster. When we got back, the saloon bar door was hospitably ajar. M. Crapoule greeted us with some suspicion and a lot of teeth-clicking. 'You weren't expected this early you know. We're usually busy at this time, preparing for the evening. You can't cook on this scale at a moment's notice. We'd better find out if you're booked in first. What name was it ... Well, there's no Cooper here. There's the Tite-Evanses, Lady Rapping and party, Mr and Mrs Sefton-Strangeley, Dr Crunch from the university and the Gonders. I'm very sorry but you must have mistaken the day.'

'But we booked in June by 'phone. You were ...'

'Ah, now wait a minute. What name did you give? You could be the Gonders to think of it. D. Gonder? Yes, well you'd better take your things up. You're down for 7.45 – sharp.'

At seven o'clock we came down to the bar where M. Crapoule was polishing glasses and making idiosyncratic remarks to the room at large:

'We had a woman here last night in a party that ordered steak. When they arrived, she said she wanted her steak well done. I had to tell her that if she wanted well done steak, she must go elsewhere. There's only one way to cook a steak and that's the only way we serve it.'

We all gave murmurs of appreciation. Crapoule delved a little deeper into his memoirs:

'Like the woman who came here with her husband and Madame had done them a beautiful meal with tiny new kidney potatoes. Just as I was about to put some on her plate, she waved them aside. "No potatoes for me", she said. "I'm slimming." Well, I told her, there's no point in coming to Puddingly if you're slimming. I gave her a double helping and stood over her while she ate them.'

We shifted in our seats and tried to give the impression that we'd eat anything honest Yves cared to set before us.

'Yes, I've had some people here. Mind, they only come once. I had a bishop here one night. Lit a pipe in my dining-room. "One moment, my lord," I said, "I wouldn't smoke in your holy place and I'd be obliged if you wouldn't smoke in mine." He hasn't been back either!'

After a few moments Crapoule disappeared and effected an entrance down a flight of stairs. 'Lady Rapping, it's ten past seven. Your party please, otherwise the *poitrine d'agneau panée* will become limp.' With little cries of delight and excitement, Lady Rappin and her party tripped up the stairs. At half past there were more alarms and excursions, and the Tite-Evanses were shepherded aloft for their *côtes de porc à la Bayonnaise* which were at that moment approaching the peak of gastronomic perfection. The similarity between the bar and a doctor's waiting room was heightened by the white coat and heavy black, psychiatrist's glasses which Crapoule had donned. At seven forty-five precisely the Gonders were summoned. I must say the Sefton-Strangeleys looked at us warily as we went aloft. ('Do you think they're Armenian, dear? Must say it's a damned funny name!')
As we entered the Temple of Gastronomy, Crapoule explained that a dish such as we had ordered, *hachis de boeuf à la purée de pomme de terre*, although simple in appearance, was more difficult to prepare than other dishes as the meat had to be – the right word escaped him, but by making a small O with

the thumb and forefinger of his left hand and expelling a
'fttt'! sound through ballooning lips, we got the idea –
we had set Madame Crapoule a Herculean labour. As we
had been looking forward to *tournedos Bordelaise*, the edge was
slightly taken off our appetite. With flourishes from the
Crapoule family we were seated, candles were lit, tureens of
butter and crisp french bread set before us and the first
course arrived. The *purée de gibier* was every bit as good as
Baxter's Game Soup. In fact, as we sat waiting for Crapoule's
next extravagance and toying with the modest bottle of wine
that I had thought appropriate to be drunk with beef hash
and mashed, we formed the opinion that it probably *was*
Baxter's Game Soup.

I must say the hash was very tasty, and the cheeseboard was
like something out of the back end of the *Observer* supplement.

'Would Madame like her Cheddar, Wensleydale, Stilton,
double Gloucester, Welsh mountain goat cheese or does she
prefer her Continental board – Bleu de Basillac, Cantal,
Epoisses, Récollet de Gerardmar, Stracchino?'

We chose our cheese, and I asked for the apple-board.

'I'm sorry, sir, we have no apples – if you'd wanted fruit you
should have ordered at the time, sir. This is not an ordinary
restaurant. All our food is prepared to order.'

Crapoule was looking challenging. Perhaps it was the way I'd
asked for that very ordinary wine to go with the beef hash.
Had I been marked down as one of nature's malcontents, a
troublemaker, a chap who finds fault?

'If Monsieur isn't satisfied with the meal, there is no obligation
to pay. We have very high standards here, and I would
rather have no customers than dissatisfied customers...'

A high-pitched note was entering Crapoule's voice.

I wasn't complaining, I said, I was only asking if I could

have an apple with my cheese. I always have an apple with my cheese. Good grief, after all . . .'

A high-pitched note was entering my voice too. The situation was saved by one of Crapoule's nephews dropping something hot and runny on the floor. The rage was directed elsewhere. The bill, when it came, was very reasonable – £4 9s 3d. We shan't be going there again. Not because we didn't genuinely enjoy the game soup and beef hash and mashed potatoes and the cheese and coffee. It was the physical exhaustion that the process involved, but as we heard Crapoule say to the Sefton-Strangeleys: 'Eating is not only a pleasure, Monsieur, it is a privilege. You have to work hard at it. No success is achieved without effort.' We're not going to make the effort again.

CASE EIGHT   Just as this book was going to press a journalist who spends most of his life travelling round Britain rang me in the small hours of the morning from a hotel in Yorkshire. Translated into received English what he said was, 'Would you like a short report on the worst hotel in Britain, written by an expert on the subject?' I said yes, and four days later a thick envelope fell on the mat with a note which said, 'Every word of this is absolutely true. May God help us all!' The hotel itself appears in the current *Good Food Guide*, it has 18 rooms and belongs to a large chain. Here is the report:

'Inured as all travellers must be to the bloody-mindedness accorded to guests at many British hotels, I was still mildly surprised as my secretary pushed open the doors with her cases to see the white-coated, immaculately creased hall porter watch her with appreciation but utter indifference. He continued to stand watching, but with less appreciation, as I followed her through the doors with my own luggage. We registered. When I asked if we could have dinner straight away we were told that dinner finished at 8.30. The time on the clock was exactly 8.31. When I protested there was a lengthy dispute which ended in consultations with the management and a grudging decision: "You can have something cold like a salad with ham or turkey."

By this time it was 8.40. The porter was summoned and, moved by the word of the manager, not only showed us to our rooms but *carried our bags*. I had already seen a prominent notice saying that 10% service charge would be added to the bill automatically, and this made him a pretty lucky man in my book.

After a further inconvenience which I imposed by ringing-up my wife, we found the restaurant. The last four diners were halfway through their main course. It must have been fully 8.50. Two plates of turkey were laid out with bowls of rather attenuated salad. As it was a cold night I asked if we might have soup. We could. The waitress sighed, disappeared and came back with two bowls of soup. We ate rapidly, cringingly. We had caught up with the other diners who were allowed a chocolate ice each, despite the fact that it was fully nine o'clock. I asked for two ices and was refused. I pointed out that the other diners had just been served with ices. The head-waitress then began a loud homily, the main points of which I summarize: she hoped I would live another 25 years because by that time there would be no service at all in any British hotels. Everything would be self-service. The only people in Britain who would work in our hotels were foreigners whose countries were in any case too poor to pay them a living wage. She worked from 7 a.m. to 10 p.m. with a two hour afternoon break to look after two children and an invalid dad – all for £5 per week. She had seen us all "including commercials" and knew that nobody would pay any more for better service.

I said I sympathized; that I knew about the iniquities of catering wages, but had eaten far beyond city limits in the USA, Germany, France, Holland, Belgium, Italy, Yugoslavia, Norway, Denmark and Sweden, where the starving waiters had nonetheless managed to give me, grinning through their hunger, the impression that it was a pleasure to serve my dinner at times up to 11 p.m. and beyond, but no doubt this was part of their tradition of smiling through their troubles, which was quite alien to us. So why didn't she and her colleagues demand higher wages for shorter hours and a double shift system, for which I would gladly pay more to get a *good* dinner at 8.31 and even the chance of a sweet at 9 p.m.

"You don't know," she said, "how the other half live." (Untrue. I have belonged to the other half for many years. That is why I stay in hotels like this one.)

We could however have coffee in the lounge outside. In the warm, spring evening the lounge had developed a damp but biting chill. By the reception desk we found a coal fire. Coffee was served under the nose of the manager. At 10.45 he put out all the lights. By the flickering fire we read a restrictive practices notice informing us that there was no night porter: obviously we all had to be driven to bed somehow.

We felt our way up the stairs. The way to my room led along four corridors, each in total darkness. Each was blocked by a glass door and punctuated by flights of stairs. I groped for all the light switches and to save myself personal injury left them all on in all the corridors. I suppose this was an act of unpardonable spitefulness.

The morning tea arrived with the *Daily Telegraph*. I dressed, walked across the square and bought the *Guardian* without difficulty. It was the paper I had ordered. The bill for one mediocre room (with no services beyond a wash basin), breakfast, dinner, morning tea and my least favourite paper came to £2 12s 5d – to it was added the "service charge".

As I left my room, carrying my own luggage, the Bible thoughtfully provided lay on the table, on its cover was stamped, "Please leave in a prominent place because the next guest may need it." I hoped he would find The Way, not to mention Truth – but I'm still not certain about the Light.'

On stage

Visitors to the newly re-opened restaurant were particularly
impressed with the gay decorations. The South Sea Island
motif, with palm trees, tropical fish in tanks, native basketwork
and 'thatched' roof bar, is a truly delightful setting. The
waitresses in their hula skirts lend an authentic touch to this
gay new nightspot. Hawaiian music is discreet and the diner
is transported thousands of miles away by the ingenuity of it
all. Well done, says the *Herald*.

Local paper report of restaurant opening, June, 1966

It's possible to eat very well in a simple room and very badly in an expensively decorated room. But, however good the food is, your enjoyment isn't going to be improved if you actively dislike the way the walls have been painted or the strange costume the waitress has got herself up in.

I used to enjoy visiting a small hotel in Scotland, but I found my interest dwindling when the new owner built himself what he called 'The Tartan Bar' and where, against a background of clan colours and antlers, he now presides in kilt and sporran – watched with rightful suspicion by the natives. It's not really his wife with her plaid trousers and Negronis that puts my back up, but what they've done to a once pleasant hotel.

Is there perhaps some streak of fantasy inside every restaurateur waiting to spring out in a riot of extravagance? I was in a café in Bristol recently which specialized in grills and cold meat and salads. On the walls were no less than 16 different kinds of wall-covering; a great rash of illuminated signs directed your attention to the GENTS, EMERGENCY EXIT, TRY OUR QUIK-SNAX; each table had its bowl of plastic flowers and the proprietor was on a step ladder hanging up cardboard lanterns from which artificial illuminated roses trailed.

Every penny of profit was being ploughed back in maniac flights of fancy; painted trellis, quilted plastic, anything perhaps to take your mind off the food. In Britain it's almost mandatory that the smaller restaurant or café should fall into one of five categories: nautical, homespun, Mediterranean, traditional or utilitarian.

THE LOBSTER POT

Sometimes known, particularly in Cornwall, as THE SMUGGLER'S DEN or THE PIRATE'S COVE. In other parts of the country it may appear as THE CAPTAIN'S CABIN, THE FISHING SMACK, THE SHIP'S LANTERN, FISHERMAN'S REST

or THE OLDE WHARF. Fishing nets hang from ceiling and walls, green glass floats are arranged 'decoratively', there is simulated rock wall paper and a few marine objects scattered about – a ship's wheel, a binnacle, the empty shells of sea urchins, port and starboard lights. Spanish wicker-work lobsters hang on the wall or perhaps crawl out of genuine lobster pots. Chairs are often formed out of barrels. Note the prints of sailing ships, aquaria and portholes of opaque glass lit from behind. The staff are often dressed in yachting clothes with the name of the restaurant woven into their jerseys. The owner may wear a cap at a rakish angle and sport a Hemingway grizzle. Menu has a nautical flavour, saucy mermaids, wreathed rope, fish with winking eye. Possible

danger of piped nautical music, lavatories being labelled
'Mermaids and Mermen' or 'Lubbers and Lasses'. Although
this kind of restaurant is most frequently found in small spoilt
fishing villages, nautical whimsy is met inland as well.

ANNE'S PANTRY

Found all over England, but appears to flourish most strongly
in market and cathedral towns and in the Home Counties.
Key names are THE CRINOLINE LADY, THE BUSY BEE,
THE COPPER KETTLE. Many of these restaurants and tea
rooms are named after flowers, LAVENDER BLUE,
MARIGOLD TEA ROOMS, THE SWEET PEA. Recurrent
adjectives: TUDOR and ELIZABETHAN. Anything which
smacks of a nice pot of tea and/or home comfort can be
used: THE SUGAR BOWL, ONE FOR THE POT, THE
SPINNING WHEEL, THE BEEHIVE, THE HONEYPOT.
Variations are played here with the addition of YE OLDE –
it seems anything pre-1930 can legitimately be YE OLDE.

Usually run by one or more ladies with names like Ruth or
Helen and professional-class accents. Smocks are worn, lisle
stockings and sensible shoes.

Look out for little brass bells on the tables to summon
attention, handwritten menus, line drawings of cathedrals,
oak settles, wheelback chairs, polished wood floors, folk-weave
mats and leaded windows. Predominant colours black and
cream, or washed-out blues and greens.

Impression given that Ruth and Helen are only really doing
this because they have to and they'd much rather be out
prison-visiting or arranging flowers on the nearest altar.

Prices are either surprisingly low or surprisingly high, portions
consistently small. There are usually short poems on the walls
about the virtues of a garden in the summer, friendship
with animals, or the rewards attained by constant humility.
As the social status of Ruth and Helen is ambivalent they get
few tips, but one is never sure whether they're pleased about
this or a bit narked. Helen and Ruth often sell things to
help out: unstamped brown eggs, home-made marrow jam,
glass animals, herbal remedies, hand-woven cloth, dried
bananas and nut products.

CASA BLANCA

Casa anything, for that matter. Anything, in fact, which
stimulates the appetite by association. Directed to the
increasingly large number of people who have been south to
the sun and retain memories of pleasant Italian or Spanish
food. THE SPANISH GRILL, EL this or that, or the addition,
of the words RISTORANTE, ALBERGO or TRATTORIA are an
excuse for a vaguely Mediterranean décor. Predominant
colours here are rich blues and warm pinks. THE CAPRI
may have grotto murals painted by a student at the local
technical college; IL MARE, a photo blow-up of the harbour
at Portofino. Lattice work is almost essential, either to divide
one part of the restaurant from another or as an anchorage

from which to hang bunches of red and white plastic grapes
and oranges and lemons. Bull fighting posters, Spanish hats,
and pieces of Mediterranean pottery complete, or perhaps
dispel, the illusion. The casa is lit from the ceiling by
fluorescent strip, but each table has its individual candle in
a Chianti bottle. Salt and pepper are often in miniature
Chianti bottles.

Whereas the Anne's Pantry type restaurant looks better by
day than at night, these restaurants are better visited when it
is dark. With sunlight pouring in, the shabbiness and
do-it-yourself décor looks raffish to say the least.

THE DOURLY ARMS

A large number of restaurants in Britain are contained in
hotels. In many small towns and villages the only place
where you can get a meal other than fish and chips or a
snack-on-toast is in what used to be the local coaching inn.

The dining-rooms of these hotels have an almost uncanny similarity – which is perhaps not so remarkable when you realize that they may be owned by the same brewery or belong to some national catering chain and many of them share an aura of crumbling decay. Before eating, one might visit the Cocktail Lounge. This is high-ceilinged, draughty and warmed in winter by a faint glow from one bar of an ancient electric fire. There are Victorian sporting prints on the wall, and a very old barman who keeps getting confused. He wages a losing battle with the wine waiter who is in and out, tapping with his tray on the counter and asking for Light Ales and half bottles of Spanish Burgundy. The carpet is usually threadbare and the occasional tables rickety. The dining-room itself will be two or three times as high as it is long, cream paintwork being set off by acres of beige embossed wallpaper with a fancy 'dado'.

If the hotel is part of a chain, there will be Kodachrome enlargements of sister establishments on the wall. There will be a selection of bottled wines on the mantlepiece and a great sideboard in the corner with a few pieces of blackened silver on display. The linen will be relatively spotless but heavily darned. The ambiance of such a room is almost indescribable – there are overtones of the dentist's waiting room and a bygone luxury when they used to burn two hundredweight of coal a week in the fire, long since boarded up.

THE GAY ADVENTURE

I suppose there are thousands of these all over the country. They are the basic cheap-quick eatery. It could be PAM'S CAFE or THE SILVER COIN or THE CHEQUER-BOARD or any of a thousand 'that'll do' names. It's most probably double-fronted; net curtains and steamed up windows mercifully conceal what goes on inside. There will probably be advertisements for some aerated drink made with chemicals or an aspirin product, and a menu, or even a sandwich-board, outside. Inside there is an impression of height, regularity, (all the tables and chairs are probably tubular and arranged in formal rows,) and bleakness. At the back, a long counter with some steaming apparatus, probably a tea urn. In a place of honour will be a large white ice-box from which are dispensed scoops of ice-cream to go on the tinned peaches. The waitresses are young and more interested in gossip with each other than attending to the customers, and the walls are conspicuously bare of decoration, except perhaps for an advertisement for Coca-Cola or Envoy Cigarettes. On the door hangs a black and white cardboard notice with the legend CLOSED on one side and OPEN on the other. There is a strong smell of food here, a mixture of frying and steam. Children abound.

Anne's Pantry, The Lobster Pot, Casa Blanca, The Dourly Arms and The Gay Adventure are not the end of the story. There are other specialized eating places with which we deal elsewhere. But while we're discussing how places look, we ought to examine a fairly new phenomenon born in post-war London but rapidly spreading to provincial cities. The concept behind these restaurants is that you should be led to believe you are eating not in a restaurant but in the hold of a tea clipper or an army mess, or an eighteenth-century chop-house, or an antique shop specializing in the sale of ear trumpets. Instead of taking a few imaginary examples, one might just as well look at some recent real examples of decorative fantasy.

There's the Maze Coffee House in the Royal Garden Hotel which has been designed to recapture the atmosphere of a garden in Tudor times. There's the Showboat in Lyons Strand Corner House, (which, by the way, cost £100,000 or enough to give 1,000 old age pensioners coffee and a biscuit every day for 5 years) loosely modelled on a Mississippi showboat. The décor includes paddle wheels churning water on either side of the cabaret stage and simulated ships' timbers.

The Kentucky Palace Pancake Kitchen in Oxford Street has a nigger minstrel motif, but Flanagan's in Baker Street went way out when it opened. The wine waiter was a chimpanzee, a move the implications of which, both for the clientele and the management, still make the mind boggle. Lyons have decorated one of their recent ventures with 240 hand-forged fencing blades, handcrafted for them by the famed sword makers, Wilkinson's. Although they may not stimulate digestion, presumably they could promote some kind of dialogue between two people who otherwise would have nothing to say to each other.

SHE   Are those swords on the wall?
HE   Well, they look like it, don't they – funny place to hang 240 hand-forged fencing blades.
SHE   Is that what they are – hand-forged fencing blades?
HE   I expect so – something like that.
SHE   Well, I wonder what they'll get up to next?

HE   Well, they might put sawdust on the floor, have bits of old motor cars stuck to the walls, and dress the waiters in caps and goggles.

SHE   Ooh, that's a smashing idea.

HE   Yes, that's what a man called Stephen Kennedy thought. He's done that at his latest restaurant in Bishopsgate.

SHE   I wonder what he's called it?

HE   The Two Hoots!

SHE   That's a terrific name for a vintage car restaurant, isn't it? I mean, it's so atmospherey. But what sort of food would you serve in a place like that?

HE   Boiled beef and carrots with pease pudding and dumplings, and for afters baked jam roll and custard.

SHE   But that's what we have at home, that's cheap food.

HE   Well, you can get it out now, only it's no longer cheap.

SHE   Have you got any more ideas for taking people's minds off eating?

HE   Well, if you got a lot of converted treadle-operated sewing machine tables and a lot of busbies, bugles, lances, trumpets and cannon, you could call it the Charge of the Light Brigade.

SHE   Why don't *we* open a restaurant like that?

HE   Somebody already has. And what's more *they've* got sawdust on the floor too, and they've also got a notice asking you to refrain from expectorating on the menu.

SHE   Ooh, what a giggle. I'd much rather have gone there. It's only silly old swords here.

HE   If you opened a fish restaurant and got it up with scallop shells and nets, you could dispense with the cover charge.

SHE   How do you know?

HE   Well, Lyons have done that. They've got one called The Fisherman's Wharf, all got up with scallop shells and nets.

SHE   And there's no cover charge?

HE   No, no cover charge at all.

SHE   That's funny.

HE   Yes, they call it a Mooring Charge!

SHE   That's a giggle. (*They both laugh uncontrollably*). You could have a fish restaurant called the Hook, Line and Sinker and have a lot of those nice coloured fly things on show.

HE   You've been cheating – you've been down Baker Street!

SHE   Well, I can't think of anything new.

HE   I can. How's this for something really sprauncy? Get the Rt. Hon. Peter Thorneycroft, sometime Minister for Defence, noted member of the Army and Navy Club and versatile Old Etonian –

SHE   Yes –

HE   – get him to do some painted panels depicting London scenes, and then get a large marble statue of Diana, Goddess of Hunting, six stained glass windows, a splendid wrought-iron screen, coats of arms, stuffed animals (especially birds), a lot of waiters dressed as footmen and eighteenth-century portraits dark with age –

SHE   Sounds a bit creepy. What's it got up to be, then?

HE   Well, I'd've thought that was obvious. You see, it's the atmosphere of a country house we're after there, rather than a restaurant.

SHE   What would you call it, then?

HE   Oh, it's too late. It's been done. They call it The Hunting Lodge, or something.

SHE   Haven't they got any hand-forged swords?

HE   No.

SHE   (*Collecting her things*) Well, that's something, isn't it?

The remarkable thing about a restaurant should be its food. The place itself should be cool in summer, warm in winter.

If there's a pleasant view through the windows, so much the better. But there's a mistaken notion going the rounds that by dressing the waiters up in Trappist habits or engraving the wine list on a parchment scroll, the meal will in some way be better. There is a tendency too for the extravagances of the décor to overflow into the menu. In the Merry Go Round in Leicester Square, where the waitresses wear bustles and the waiters striped waistcoats, the 'Bill of Fayre' burbles about 'our very bespoke Bread and Butter pudding' and 'Rich Chicken Broth to warm the Cockles of your Heart'. The most expensive item on the menu is described like this: 'FOR SALE (Semi-detached, Suit Any Couple) A luvverly, beautiful, whole Chicken, for two. Carefully cooked over a log-fire in a Cauldron, filled with an enriched stock of choice Vegetables, Exotic Herbs, Peppers – and lots of luscious Things. Served with braised Rice and rich Cream sauce. "Ye will hae tae bide a wee while". ' The wine list is equally witty and contains such facetious entries as 'Really Sophisticated Brandies from the district of Cognac', 'Aulde Whiskys from Bonny Scotland' and 'Many Liqueurs as Brewed by Witches and Abbots of Olde'. Several interior decorators have gone on record as saying that a meal in a restaurant should be a 'dramatic experience'. Drama does, of course, sometimes arise unexpectedly. Like the April evening in 1962 when a friendly guest threw a biscuit to the 5ft Indian cayman, who is one of the props in the Beachcomber Restaurant of the Mayfair Hotel. The alligator snapped its great jaws shut like a portcullis and trapped another prop, an edible tortoise, between its teeth. Eventually, after the alligator had got very angry, the R.S.P.C.A. were called in and Mike Chester, one of their workers, leapt into the pool in waders and struggled for 30 minutes, trying to get a noose over the alligator's head. There's drama if you want it.

And if you want sexual thrills when you eat out – London used to supply that as well. In the early sixties there was a restaurant in Bayswater where you could watch a naked girl while you ate. The idea was that art students could eat and work at the same time. According to the *News of the World*: 'Many middle-aged men, who have never drawn before, now spend hours drawing away for all they are worth'.

SHE Well eat up then.

HE What did you say – ?

SHE What do you keep looking through me for? It's as if I wasn't here.

HE I was just looking at the fittings, that's all.

SHE You can't keep your eyes off HER, can you!

HE Well, it is a bit unusual, I must say . . . it's the first time I've eaten tinned fruit salad in the presence of a stark naked lady.

SHE Now I know why you were so solicitous about my sitting facing the wall. It's a wonder someone doesn't throw her a bun.

HE She looks quite a nice class of girl from what you can see.

SHE I'd've thought from the way you've been squinting and straining all through your honeydew melon and chicken kebab, that you've seen more than most.

HE It's a wonder, really, they didn't think of it before.

SHE I feel absolutely silly sitting here, the only woman in the room.

HE Well, you're not the *only* woman in the room, dear.

SHE Well, I'm the only one with any clothes on. Give me hand-forged fencing blades any day – and I don't want coffee either!

The catering industry has come to subscribe to the theory that people going to restaurants nowadays want to be entertained. 'They don't want a bare room. They want pleasant surroundings, something unusual – something out of the way.'
And it seems that caterers are bending over all ways to give

it to them. For instance, in Ind Coope's Piccadilly Hotel in Manchester, there are three unusual rooms. King Arthur's Court banqueting suite, the King Cotton bar, and the Peacock room. The rooms in King Arthur's Court create the impression of sitting in a large tent. Drapes of glass fibre cloth, lit from behind, give the effect of sunshine. The curtain pelmets are rows of helmets, and on the walls are jousting spurs and heraldic shields.

Of the Golden Egg restaurants, currently the most successful innovation in British catering, a spokesman said, 'They are humorous, gay and entertaining, like a stage set'. At the time of writing, the latest trend materials are 'Perspex for coloured ceiling light boxes, moulded Polystyrene, and multi-coloured fused glass walls'.

All this decoration is not cheap. A contemporary steakhouse will cost between £20,000 and £40,000 to design, furnish and equip. Dennis Lennon, the man responsible for all those hand-forged fencing blades, also designed the Double Time coffee shop in the Cumberland Hotel. He incorporated 20 clocks in the décor: 'People immediately start talking about the clocks when they come into the room'. Success! When the owners of the Northcliffe Hotel in Brixham spent £30,000 improving their Devon hotel, they installed the 'Barnacle Bar'. Its atmosphere is a combination of tropical and marine, with a ceiling covered in bamboo cane and hundreds of sea shells and bottle ends embedded in the walls. In the El Bodega, puddings appear in bed pans; at the Tiberio, they incorporated seven tons of lava from Vesuvius in the décor. The latest development comes from a firm called Décor Extraordinaire who have introduced do-it-yourself kits for converting your restaurant into a swinging scene. Prices range from £150 to £1,150. The Bali Hai kit which costs just under £300 offers you a nine-foot palm tree with six fronds, three tropical plants, ten coloured plants, twelve illuminated tropical flowers, two large creepers, four warrior shields, ten warrior spears, five illuminated masks, three

ordinary masks and 200 yards of fluorescent coloured trails –
all fireproof. And so it goes zanily on. As one leading restaurant
designer said, 'I see my restaurants as a stage set, the
customers are the actors.'

All this is a far cry from days when you went out to get
something to eat. Eating has now become a dramatic
experience, a happening. One feels that it might not be long
before some of the more theatrical restaurants insist on a
two-year course at a reputable drama school before letting
you in.

Even the Church has begun to take notice of this new social
revolution. It was on the 5th December, 1961, that then
Suffragan Bishop of Kensington, the Rt. Rev. Cyril Easthaugh
made catering history. When the Park Gate Hotel in
Bayswater Road re-opened after re-decorating and furnishing,
he was in attendance to sanctify the face-lift with an episcopal
blessing.

Behind the scenes

'When I first got into the industry and saw what went on, I decided well, this really wasn't for me – you know. If I've got to dish this stuff up I've got to dish this stuff up, but I'm certainly not going to have to eat it, and I decided not to eat in restaurants. But this didn't last long'

A sous-chef in a London hotel

Most people, on going out for a meal, assume that the standard of cleanliness attained in the restaurant where they are eating is as high, if not higher, than it would be at home. Alas, this is not always so. But we remain a nation of incorrigible and pathetically hopeful optimists. What is perhaps alarming is not the occasional prosecution for keeping a filthy kitchen, but the dangers to health in kitchen techniques which are standard practice up and down the country – techniques which are actively encouraged by advertising. The Food Editor of *The Hotel and Catering Times* felt so strongly about these practices that she recently warned her readers:

'The bacterial danger that lurks behind headlines exhorting pub caterers to use up left-over hot snacks in imaginative Eastern dishes is enough to turn a hygiene officer in his grave. Readers should be guarded before conning ideas from these recipes. Publicity officers, who are experts in the field of domestic cookery, pressure them on catering Press editors. And some less informed sources use them. Beware!'

She might well be worried.
At the beginning of 1966 Dr J. F. E. Bloss, Senior Medical Officer in the Ministry of Health, speaking at a conference on food hygiene, pointed out the dangers in pre-cooking prepared meat dishes like stews, steak and kidney pies and shepherd's pie:

'Scientific experiment has shown that if this practice is necessary, it should only be carried out provided the kitchen staff can take the proper precautions . . . . the practice can only be justified if the kitchen has an efficient larder and the procedure is closely supervised. To cool the meat down in the warm kitchen encourages the organisms to multiply, and to re-heat slowly to a temperature which is only warm produces a temperature favourable to bacterial growth.'

Despite warnings like these from medical men and responsible

71

people in the industry, and despite the knowledge that re-heating causes 40% of all the reported cases of food poisoning in Britain, the re-heating of pre-cooked food under conditions which could lead to the spread of disease is part and parcel of food preparation in all but a few kitchens. When *The People* carried out a public health survey in the summer of 1965, they didn't have to hunt about to find the evidence. One restaurant owner wrote from the north:

'Recently we had to provide a roast beef lunch for 400 children and 40 adults at 12.30 p.m. I fail to see how we could have done this if we hadn't cooked the beef the day before . . .'

The letter went on to explain that shortly before the party arrived, the meat was sliced and then put on 'very hot dinner plates to which piping-hot fresh gravy was added'. This disarmingly frank admission does help to explain why so much of the meat eaten in hotels and restaurants in this country tastes as if it were sliced cold, put on very hot dinner plates and covered with piping-hot fresh gravy.
It may be necessary to pre-cook meat, but it's also gratifyingly economic – meat sliced cold goes further than meat sliced hot. And when you're dishing up cold meat and hot gravy on a big scale, it goes even further when the joint is put in a bacon slicer – that's the way to get it really razor thin; so thin that if you hold it up to a window on a dull summer's day you can see the sun glinting faintly through it.
Filth in homes and restaurants and the factories where food is prepared causes over 60 known cases of food poisoning a week. Some of the filth occurs in the mass preparation of food. A box of matches turned up in a tin of pears, a rifle slug in a tin of steak, a signet ring in a chunk of luncheon meat, a beetle and a wad of chewing-gum in a jar of processed apples. A bakery was fined £35 after a half-inch screw was found in a bun. In 1964 alone Public Health Inspectors investigated more than 3,750 cases of 'foreign bodies' in food in England and Wales.

72

The visitations of our Public Health inspectors and the
subsequent prosecutions make grim reading. There was the
restaurant where the inspector found 'cockroaches, cobwebs,
flaky walls, dirty cooking equipment and greyish meat which
gave off a sour odour'. There was a £100 fine for that.
At the time of the Aberdeen typhoid outbreak, the Labour
M.P. for Coatbridge and Airdrie said in the House of
Commons: 'Thousands of people who are taking meals from
certain restaurants would not dream of consuming them if
they knew the unhygienic conditions under which they were
cooked' and he was not exaggerating. Most Americans,
when they visit this country for the first time, are either
shocked or repelled by our casual attitude to hygiene – the

way dogs are allowed in restaurants, cats curl up on kitchen tables and food is prepared in mediaeval conditions. English people can be shocked too; this was a recent letter in the *Daily Telegraph*:

'A friend and I went into a Soho restaurant and ordered a meal. As I had arrived in a hurry and wanted a wash and brush up before eating, I was directed to the nether regions and *en route* had to pass through the kitchen, where a chef and several assistants were busy about their work. I suddenly noticed, in the centre of the kitchen, a large oblong open container full of pre-cooked chips, no doubt awaiting 'chipping up' as and when required in the restaurant. On top of the chips reclined a large, well-fed cat, fast asleep. Needless to say, we dined elsewhere.'

One of the folk legends in my wife's family is the occasion when her father and mother were returning home for their annual leave. In Cairo they were tempted by a street stall of juicy, glistening strawberries, dew-fresh, dawn-chilled as the switched-on menus would say. But they were slightly put off when, on turning the corner, they found the proprietor's ancient uncle 'freshening' the berries one at a time in his mouth. Of course, that sort of thing could only happen in Cairo! Or could it? Here's Bob Wynn writing in the *Daily Worker*, September, 1964:

'I'm partial to apples, as most of my friends know. And I reckon I must be as experienced an apple buyer as anyone, but I got a shock when I went rather early to my favourite market stall the other day. The stall-holder was busy polishing some apples. He spat on them first, and then polished them on his handkerchief.'

We English are always going into pubs or restaurants and seeing things we shouldn't – and rushing into print about them too:

'A friend and I had a long and tiring business day and, at the

point where our roads divided, went in for a parting glass of of beer. There were, on the bar, some tempting-looking sandwiches, carefully under cover with tongs for serving, but the door at the back of the bar into the kitchen was open. There, on the table, which was obviously used for the preparation of food, was lying a large dog. We asked the manageress whether the sandwiches had been cut in the kitchen and, on her assurance that they had, thanked her and said we did not want them and invited her to look at the dog. She gave one horrified glance and then marched into the kitchen. We were quite speechless when we heard her shout at the chef "How many times have I told you to keep this door shut?" '

That letter appeared in the *Daily Telegraph* not so long ago. By the way, you might think that this was an isolated incident.

But only 33 days later Bob Wynn was regaling his *Daily Worker* readers with an uncannily similar experience:

'Only the other day I was in a Manchester café, where the counter formed a sort of frontier between two worlds. All was spotless on the customers' side, but I noticed through an open door that everything was scruffy in the kitchen beyond. In the kitchen was a dog which, between scratching himself for fleas, licked a tray of cream buns standing on a box six inches from the floor. I pointed this out to a woman behind the counter. She said not a word to me but, livid with anger, turned to the kitchen and shouted, "Fred, how many more times have I got to tell you to keep that door shut?"'

A dog in the kitchen is so obvious a health hazard that most people would resent it. But what about the potential dangers to health which the layman isn't aware of? What about those little plastic flags which some restaurants stick in their steaks, when they bring them to the table? What about the little plastic labels stuck into pies and sandwiches on pub counters? Recently Dr W. G. Swann, Medical Officer of Health for the Port and City of London said, during the course of what I found a most disturbing lecture, 'Enquiries made by my staff seem to indicate that little attention is paid to any method of cleaning and sterilizing this type of label, and yet there seems to be great reluctance to abandon them even when it has been proved that the mould growth in their produce arises as a direct result of these practices'.

I was so impressed with this intelligence that next time I went into a pub which had these little flags stuck in the sandwiches I retailed Dr Swann's theories as entertainingly as I could to the landlord. The reply was indignant: 'That's a lot of rot! We sell fifty rounds of sandwiches a day and they're all freshly made. They don't know nothing about it. They want to come and work here. This place is bloody spotless. Look at that brass up there polished every day of the year 'cept Sundays.' With a gesture of contempt he wrung out a filthy cloth in the washing-up water, ostentatiously wiped the counter all round my glass, stubbed out his fag and stalked off to the other end of the bar. A few minutes later I watched him pick out a cheese sandwich from the display case using the plastic tongs with mannered daintiness. He placed the sandwich on an old chopping-board and pressing it flat with a nicotine-stained hand cut it in half.

I reckon Dr Swann could have based a whole course of lectures on a few lunchtime visits to that pub. All the makings of an epidemic were scattered round the bar: lukewarm shepherd's pie made from a left-over joint of beef, pork pie kept just warm enough on a hotplate to foster the growth of bacteria, a sink of permanently unchanged cold water in which the glasses were swilled out, the barman's hand going constantly from food, to fag, to mouth, and back to food. If they ever launch a Keep Britain Filthy movement they might well do worse than set up their headquarters by the snack counter of the nearest local.

If bacteria could be seen, it would make life much easier. But the chef who works with dirty finger-nails, or the waitress who scratches her head and then daintily arranges the cakes, cannot see the trail of infection they're laying like a fuse. Now and again someone blows their top and then all the restaurateurs get angry. Like the day in October 1954 when Mr Donald Chapman, Socialist M.P. for Northfield, rose in the House of Commons and said that he had got to the stage where there was practically no restaurant in Soho where he could bear to eat 'so dirty are the things which people wear when they come to serve me. If they are dirty when they serve me at table, consider how much dirt there is behind the scenes'. An invitation which drew angry howls of denial from Soho.

Lady Lewisham launched an attack on Britain's 'sordid and disgusting kitchens' when she was opening a food research laboratory back in 1959. 'The list of food horrors,' she proclaimed, 'is endless – contaminated milk, condemned meat, iced-lollies containing dangerous deposits of lead . . . let us resolve to demand clean food wherever we may be.'

In 1964, the Association of Public Health Inspectors reported several strange and disturbing situations, none perhaps more bizarre than the restaurant where food was kept in a flooded cellar. The kitchen staff wore Wellingtons to wade through sewage when fetching supplies. In another case, cockroaches and cigarette ends were found in a bakehouse. Tables and trays were encrusted with dirt and flour residue, and joints half an inch wide were filled with dirt.

With over a quarter of a million public eating places in Britain, it would be strange if there weren't one or two dirty ones. But we are shockingly permissive in our attitude to dirt. There is a law which says that people shouldn't handle food and smoke at the same time. When you've seen your greengrocer having a cup of tea and a fag, and serving a pound of sprouts at the same time, have you complained? It's a law which is continually and flagrantly broken in nearly every public house in the country, and usually the landlord is the worst offender.

Everybody has their own particular list of phobias: the cracked cups and plates which are still, in the late sixties, legally acceptable; the public house glasses washed in cold water fortified with beer leavings; the steaming kitchens littered with cats and mousetraps and big jars of rancid frying oil and overflowing dustbins; the waitress's wet rag used to wipe table tops and plates and cutlery, and the fork with a dried up portion of yesterday's Dish of the Day stuck to it.

Is it really as bad as that? Well, there are those who ought to know. Like young David Tyrell, a student at Ealing Technical College Catering School. 'When I get in a position of importance, I'm going to make sure the kitchens are clean,' David told a *Sun* reporter in October 1964. 'If the public could see as I have, the floors sprinkled with dirty sawdust, the food-clogged machines which haven't been cleaned for months, they'd never eat out again.'

Perhaps it's just as well most eating places don't include a trip through the kitchen as a prelude to the evening's entertainment. There's a limit to what the human constitution can stand.

The filthy state of many hotel and restaurant kitchens is not denied, not at least by those who have to work in such conditions. One waiter told me:

'At the —— Hotel, the stench was just . . . you know, well it was unbearable. This was actually in the clearing area where we were leaving the dirty dishes. They had a porter to clear it up and send it down to the washup in the lift. And the stink in there was abominable. I never smelt a drop of anything like Dettol or any disinfectant the whole time I was there. It really used to make you feel quite sick when you walked in there . . . really a bit too much.'

A shockingly high proportion of hotels and restaurants don't provide adequate facilities for the staff to achieve the high standards of hygiene to which the industry piously pays lip-service. A contributor 'with long experience of hotel keeping and catering' told in the *Caterer and Hotel-keeper* in 1966 a 'true story by a newcomer to our business as a waitress'. The story went like this:

'Asks where to change on her first day. Shown a dirty room off the kitchen with cook's and kitchen porters' clothing hanging there too. She objects. Manager hurriedly arranges that waitresses in future will change in ladies' toilet before customers get there. This is a City of London restaurant of some repute. No wonder City Medical Officers of Health keep publishing those damning reports about hygiene in City restaurants.'

When they do exist staff changing-rooms are frequently so squalid that as one waiter put it: 'No self-respecting tramp would put his nose through the door'.

There is a tendency to believe that it's only foreign-owned

restaurants and foreign staff who have low standards of cleanliness. Hence the recurrent attacks on 'Soho' standards of hygiene. Those who share this belief will be interested in the views of an Italian, Mr Ivo Ceccavelli, on filth and dirt in British hotels and restaurants. In a letter to *The Caterer and Hotel-keeper* in 1966 he said:

'As a foreigner working in this country under permit and unable to change jobs as freely as British staff, I have read with interest recent letters on staff conditions in hotels. For instance one correspondent says, 'treat staff as human beings,' but how is this possible while many medium-sized hotels (under 100 rooms) cannot spare a room for a staff dining-room. Even among the many who do provide such a room one sees the table littered with dirty plates, dishes, cups, glasses, cigarette ends and empty packets, old newspapers and dirty clothes strewn all over the floor.'

Here is how another worker described to me the changing-room in the London hotel where he worked. The hotel is a large one with a world-wide reputation:

'I suppose the ceilings had once been white, but they were brown with filth. There were two lavatories which were utterly unusable and we used to sneak out and use the guest ones. The room itself was about the size of a suburban drawing-room, and there were 60 of us changing there. The washhand basins were covered with grime, there was a sort of black film over them . . . no, there weren't any showers or baths. Most of the doors were hanging off what lockers there were. It really made you feel like a tenth class citizen just to be in the room – made you feel physically dirty.'

I asked this man why, if he was so sensitive, he had put up with the conditions? Why hadn't he complained?

'Well, it would have been pointless. I could have said to the head-waiter who was next in the chain of authority that the conditions in the changing-room were pretty bad and he'd probably say to me: "Well, yes, we all have to work with this, don't we? But what can I do?" And if it ever did get to the General Manager, he'd probably say: "Well, I'll see about it," and that would be that, you know. The General Manager must have known that place was filthy but nothing was ever done.'

It's small wonder that unhygienic conditions breed unhygienic habits – or does it work the other way round? An employee in one of London's newest luxury hotels told me how their *commis saucier* prepared *Filet de veau à l'Italienne*:

'You may not know this dish, but it's garnished with *haricot verts*. I've watched this bloke preparing this dish and he gets these beans. He's got a handful of them and he's actually biting them down to the right size – eating the bit he's bitten off and putting the bit left into the dish. This is just about as low as you can get, but he gets away with it. I've seen him do it. Dozens of people have seen him do it, but nobody's ever said anything to him about it.'

A trainee, making his way in the industry and at the time working in a four star hotel, told me:

'A chef always has a cloth at his side. Say he has a meal, and you know chefs are not the cleanest of eaters; he'll usually end up with something dribbling down his chin, then he'll wipe his face with this cloth – the same cloth he's going to wipe a pan out with. You rarely see a chef wash his hands. And waiters – you'll quite often see them picking their noses in the servery, then a finger goes in your soup to taste it, and out it goes to you after his dirty finger's been in it.'

It seems that helping yourself to a little bit of a dish is usual practice in kitchens, either before the dish goes out or when it it comes back. One waiter told me that whitebait had a peculiar fascination behind the scenes:

B.F.G.—G

'I don't know what it is about whitebait but everybody in the hotel business seems to be keen on it. The chef'll have one or two, the waiter'll have one or two and give his friends one or two before they even get to you. By the time you get them (you'll probably have a fairly good portion) you've had a few dirty fingers going over it.'

It's obvious, I suppose, that if an order of vegetables is returned partially unconsumed, they're not going to be wasted. A waiter in a brasserie restaurant said:

'Vegetables are used again frequently. You take it to the table and somebody's probably flicked cigarette ash over it, the waiter's been sneezing on it and as it gets colder it doesn't improve and it goes back to be reheated and, of course, the more times it goes back and forth, the more awful it's getting. It's general practice to re-heat the veg.'

I collected one particularly nauseating piece of information which I have no reason to doubt is authentic. A chef described one of his colleagues at work:

'This chap's a pastry chef and nearly all pastry chefs suck their piping tubes. The thing is, if you made your royal icing or whatever it is properly, it's all very nice and smooth, but if you don't make it properly, it's full of lumps. Well, this fellow can't make it properly so there he is icing away, doing lovely work, quite the little artist, and every few moments, it goes in his mouth so that he can suck the lumps out as he goes. Oh, well, they never know out there.'

Sometimes the food itself is prepared in such a way, or is in such a condition when it's cooked, that the staff refuse to touch it. An ex-chef described a spell he'd had working last year in a large and busy restaurant which served mainly expense-account meals to businessmen – the smoked salmon, scampi, *coq au vin* touch:

'We were allowed to eat whatever we liked from the menu,

fillet steak, duck, anything. In theory, we could eat extremely well there, but we could never find anything that didn't smell as if it was going off and, in actual fact, we used to live on pints of milk and fruit and bread. I wouldn't eat there, not if you gave me a thousand pounds.'

The interesting thing is that if you talk to anyone who's had experience of industrial catering, he'll tell you that filth and dirt are not endemic there in the kitchen. As one man put it:

'The funny thing is that industrial catering is way ahead of the commercial unit. Take anywhere you like. I happen to know Hoovers, on the Western Avenue, whose standard of hygiene in their kitchen is very, very high; Marks and Spencers have an area in their kitchen where you blow your nose – if you feel a sneeze coming on, you've got to get into this area and sneeze there, away from all the food.'

Investigating hygiene in hotels and restaurants is not easy. It's not easy to get into most kitchens without an appointment. Most hoteliers and restaurateurs claim that their kitchens are spotless and impeccable. Maybe they are. There remain, as public health reports reveal, the kitchens that are frankly filthy. Why are they so dirty? I put this question to several people. One answer I got is perhaps as far as one can go:

'I'm not sure about this. If you asked them I suppose they'd tell you it boiled down to a question of economics. I don't know. They pay kitchen porters about £11 or £12 a week. Their main function at the ——— Hotel is to clean pots and pans, not so they're sterile mind, just so that they're usable. They also have to keep the floor reasonably clean so that everybody isn't slipping and sliding all over the place. But then again one suspects this is because they can be sued for damages if someone breaks their leg – rather than because of any feeling for hygiene. But I'm sure if a manager really cared about having a spotless kitchen, he could have one. I've been in some clean ones, but they're the exception.'

Anybody who's read George Orwell's stomach-turning account of working in the kitchens of a Paris hotel will know that lack of hygiene in restaurants is not confined to Britain. Certainly our industrial catering is very advanced.

Recently Marks and Spencer abolished all wood from their kitchens. They are now using stainless steel rolling pins and compressed rubber chopping boards, and they have replaced all their conventional working surfaces with plastic, tiles, or stainless steel. But that kind of hygiene costs a lot of money. If, as a nation we wanted it, I suppose we'd get it. When the Deputy Medical Officer of Health for Westminster, Dr H. Carson, said:

'I cannot emphasize too strongly my belief that education rather than enforcement is our most effective public health weapon.'

He pinpointed the heart of the problem. 'Our whole social attitude to hygiene is still primitive. When, as a society, we tolerate pavements littered with the excrement of dogs and allow animals to come into intimate contact with our food, a little bit of dirt where we can't see it, isn't likely to bother us at all.'

As one catering worker delicately phrased it.

'Let's say once you've worked in a place, you wouldn't really want to go and have a meal there, would you? If you go to a place you haven't worked in, well you haven't seen the kitchen, have you – and that's sort of encouraging. You never know it might be different from all the ones you've worked in!'

Death in the pot

'One of them went out into the field to gather herbs, and
found a wild vine and gathered from it his lap full of wild
gourds, and came and cut them up into the pot of pottage,
not knowing what they were. And they poured out for the
men to eat. But while they were eating of the pottage, they
cried out, O man of God, there is death in the pot!'

2 *Kings IV:* 39, 40

'Fifteen cases of poisoning from the nitrate in spinach eaten
by babies aged 2 to 10 months are reported in the *Lancet*
today by Dr Claus Simon, Paediatric Department, Kiel
University . . the high amount of nitrate was due to excessive
use of nitrogen fertilizer'

Report in the Daily Telegraph, *April* 1966

How safe are the food products which the catering industry is increasingly being forced to handle? It would seem from the number of health-food shops springing up that more and more men and women are becoming scared of the mass-produced product they're being offered. They pay top prices for free-range eggs, husky wholemeal bread, chickens free of hormones, apples from unsprayed trees and carrots grown in health-giving dung. When they read reports that birds of prey are being made sterile through the use of pesticides, they wonder how long it's going to be before men too begin to drop like carrion in the streets.

However unlikely this may be, and however dotty you think the food cranks are, there is an increasingly high note of hysteria in the air. You've only got to mention some new way of processing foods and the self-appointed guardians of the nation's health are showering letters into every editor's in-tray. A century or so ago the public really had more cause for alarm. In those pragmatic days they put bitter almonds in wine to give it body, coloured pickles with copper, mixed stone-dust with flour, sulphuric acid with beer, lead chromate with mustard. There was little manufactured food you could buy that was not adulterated to a greater or lesser extent. Today there's an even more widespread, if safer, use of preservatives, surfactants, anti-oxidants, emulsifiers, stabilizers, sequestrants, moisteners, colouring agents, acids, alkalis, non-nutritive sweeteners, anti-caking agents, thickeners, thinners and bleaching agents. And yet people are still surprised when they buy a food product and find a long list of chemicals among the ingredients.

Somebody went out to buy a pack of biscuits the other day and found that instead of being made of cream and butter and things like that, they were made of propyl gallate, certified colour, butylated hydroxy-toluene, mono and di-glycerides, mono-sodium glutamate, butylated hydroxyanisole, artificial flavour, cheese flavour, non-fat milk solids, cotton seed and soya oil. To find that the contents

87

also contained wheat, flour, salt, sugar and cornflour wasn't much compensation. Of course, a lot of these chemicals are found in a natural state in our food anyway, and just because we can manufacture them in laboratories doesn't suddenly make them toxic. I mean, what would a plate of chips taste like without a liberal sprinkling of sodium chloride? And if we didn't add these strange sounding substances to our food we couldn't put it in tins, and a lot of what we eat would not only be tasteless but colourless as well. On the other hand, when we find that the Food Additives and Contaminants Committee has recently totally banned butylated hydro-toluene (B.H.T.) from baby food and recommended that the amounts used in adult food should be halved . . . well, you wonder how much we know about all the other things manufacturers gaily add to their preparations to make them look, and taste, acceptable.

Should we, I wonder, be worried if there's a possibility that our bread may contain plaster, sawdust, alum, nitrogen peroxide, benzol peroxide, or calcium phosphate? In the bad old days they used to bleach our bread with agene – now they bleach it with chlorine dioxide. But how safe is that? In France and Germany bleaching agents are prohibited.

Lucky Frenchmen, lucky Germans! And even if you do ban the use of chemicals which are known to be harmful, is that the end of the story?

It was only in 1965 that the 18-year old Food Standards Committee recommended the prohibition of Coumarin, Tonka Bean, Safrole, Sassafras Oil, Dihydrosafrole, Agaric Acid, Nitrobenzene, Dulcamara, Pennyroyal Oil, Oil of Tansy, Rue Oil, Birch Tar Oil, Cade Oil, Volatile Bitter Almond Oil and Male Fern. Who knows what substances in common use today may be banned by 1975?

Five years after Rhodanine B, a bright glowing pink substance, was banned by the government, a Blackpool firm was prosecuted for continuing to make rock containing Rhodanine B. The case is disturbing, not only because it shows how easily the law can be broken, but also because it revealed that even when a substance is found to be unfit for human consumption the ban is not immediate. One of the directors of the firm claimed that they were given two years after the regulations came into force to 'clear their stocks'. This easy-going attitude may have accounted for the remark he made when told by the Chief Health Inspector that he was peddling rock containing a substance which might cause cancer. 'Haven't you got an orphanage or similar place I can give it to?'

What perhaps is worrying is our attitude to these substances we put in our food: we are quite happy to go on using them until they are definitely proved harmful, or there's a strong suspicion that they're harmful. In France, before a chemical is permitted, a case has to be made out that the addition is necessary. The French care more deeply about their stomachs than we do.

Very often, to ensure that tinned food lasts, chemicals are added which cause it to look repellent, then more chemicals have to be added to make it 'look tasty'. For instance, to make tinned peas keep in a can for as long as possible sulphur dioxide is added. But sulphur dioxide turns peas a whitish grey-green colour. To give them that emerald green colour, a drop of di-2-hydroxy-3:6 disulphonaphthyl-methanol anhydride is added. Mmm! Tasty!

To those possessed of a vivid imagination, it's a dismal picture when we look closely at it: crops growing in fields beside busy roads can become contaminated by lead additives in petrol; eating a good-sized barbecue steak, cooked over charcoal could give us as much benzpyrene (a cancer-producing substance) as smoking 700 cigarettes.

There is, too, the problem of food that's far from fresh. Not so long ago a housewife bought a packet of frozen beans in Haywards Heath, Sussex. They were described on the printed label as 'fresher than fresh'. They were four years old. During the four years, the contents through crystallization and evaporation had shrunk from ten to six ounces.

It's been said that the standard of our food today has never been better, and maybe this is true. But a documentation of the contemporary assault on standards was given by Dr H. Amphlett Williams, Public Analyst for the City of London, in an address he gave to the Royal Society of Health in 1961. He claimed that there existed 'a selection of articles which, since their name was first coined, have, in years gone by, become frequently subject to some form of debasement'. These included lemonade, cordials, orange squash, beer, custard, jam, demerara sugar, mustard, forcemeat, meat paste, French coffee, sherbet, shortbread and lemon curd. 'Unfortunately,' added Dr Williams, 'the trend does not seem to have been arrested. Since the end of the war, further traditional foods, if not already debased have been in grave danger.' He drew attention to meringues made of artificial cellulose gum, cheeses made from skimmed milk sold as cream cheese, and 'the sale under such terms as "whipped cream, Cornish cream, Jersey cream" of a grade of cream containing less fat than was usual in plain cream before the war.' Cider was sometimes sweetened with saccharin, milk bread made with skimmed milk powder. On sale were *pâté de foie* which never smelt a goose liver, and orange flavoured drinks with only 3% of orange in them. Dr Williams instanced the 'metamorphosis of the hamburger from a prime steak fried with onions into a rissole composed of preserved minced meat with cereal and onion filling, and sometimes containing only 50% of meat'. From food analysis carried out in the London area between 1955 and 1959, he gave the following instances of the percentages of samples tested which were found in some way inferior:

Fruit with lead arsenate residue	42%
Cream cheese not made from cream	35%
Bread and butter (butter was marg)	24%
Dried milk and milk foods (rancid)	20%

Dieticians are worried not so much by the possibility of our being slowly poisoned by the food technicians as by the possibility of our becoming under-nourished. It is now possible, and has been so for some time, to produce food which looks good, tastes good, but has absolutely no nutritive value whatsoever. Cheap sweets made to catch the children's market are an obvious example, so is some mass-produced ice-cream made, as it is, of sweetened lard inflated with air. In this country 40 different colourings and 400 flavours, many of them synthetic, are used in food manufacture and, with their help, it's possible to produce a whole range of food which does little more than make you feel full.

And the trend is towards a greater production of processed foods. One-fifth of a housewife's expenditure is now spent on those food products which go under the generic name of convenience foods. We might well have a closer look at them.

The age of convenience

'The manufacturer is taking over from the caterer, which will probably please both parties. Whether the public will approve is another matter'

The Hotel and Catering Times, *13th January*, 1966, *commenting on the trend towards convenience food*

Lovely Ripe Pears – Good as Tinned!

Notice outside a village General Stores

There was a story that used to be told about the Hollywood producer, who went into a drugstore and asked for a cup of coffee and a bun. 'We're fresh out of buns,' said the waitress, smiling a huge starlet's smile and squaring her shoulders. 'Well fake one!' said the producer.

It's the feeling you get in nine out of ten eating places in Britain today. That they're fresh out of anything fresh but if you'll give them a few minutes with a can, a packet, some assorted powders, a bit of dehydrated this, some heavily advertised extracts, and other substitutes, there'll be a three-course meal ready in a jiffy – and what is more there will be. Very good things come out of cans and refrigerators and packets, but the tragedy is that gradually the faked food, like a Frankenstein, is edging out the real food. Soon the only cooks will be in factories and they won't be cooks, they'll be food technicians with a detailed knowledge of chemistry. And in eating places there'll just be a few unskilled operatives thawing and re-heating. Not only will this reduce overheads and streamline the catering operation but it will also, happily, bring larger and more predictable profits. We are descending rapidly into the Age of Convenience.

Convenience foods have been described as 'processed foods for which the degree of culinary preparation has been carried to an advanced stage by the manufacturer, and which may be used as labour-saving alternatives to less highly processed products'. The caterer, faced with increasing staff shortage, is turning to them more and more.

Convenience foods have been around for a long time now. In fact, the manufacturers of Swel air-dried vegetables claim that tea, bacon, butter, smoked salmon, cheese are all forms of convenience food.

Canned products too have been with us for decades. For the lower-class trade, it is still possible to get away with canned processed peas – opening tins can be a profitable business. In 1966 one firm advertised the cost of two ounce portions of its tinned vegetables as,

baked beans	·98d
stringless beans	1·9d
baby whole carrots	1·6d
garden peas	2·0d
processed peas	1·1d
butter beans	1·4d

At a shilling a portion, you've got a profit of between 80%
and 90%.

Take soups. If you buy them in a packet they're very *convenient*
to make. To prepare a gallon of powdered soup, all you do is
'mix a packet of soup powder with 2 pints of cold water. Add
6 pints of boiling water, stirring well. Bring to the boil and
simmer for 20 minutes.' Everybody can make minestrone,
spring vegetable, oxtail or what you will as long as they can
read the simple directions on the packet. And it's all good
stuff. At Hotelympia 66 – the Hotel and Catering Exhibition,

I copied down the ingredients on a packet of tomato soup
powder. They were: dehydrated vegetables, wheat flour,
sugar, salt, potato starch, corn starch, vegetable fat,
hydrolyzed vegetable protein, spices, herbs. The average cost
of a bowl of this soup would be about 2d. One London hotel
finds them very convenient and at 4s 6d a plate is working
on a golden profit margin – mind you, that doesn't include
overheads, like the expensive tureen from which it's
generously ladled and the crisp crunchy *croûtons*.
New, and fast catching on with progressive caterers, are
'quick dried' vegetables. As one demonstrator told me, 'It's
very simple, really. While they're having their pâté or prawn
cocktail, you put a handful of these in boiling water, boil them
for ten minutes and there they are, all ready to eat. Of course
if you soak them in cold water for twenty minutes beforehand,
you get increased bulk, but it's not really necessary.'
How much more convenient, too, to be able to make your

own milk. Instead of having to wait for the milkman to come and charge you 10d a pint, you can mix your own out of a tin for less than a third the cost. And potatoes, too. You can make any amount of instant mashed potatoes for only 1½d a portion – and it requires no skill. Then there's orangeade and lemonade powder which, when made up, will cost you 0·78d per tumbler, and instant coffee powder which works out to 1s 11½d a gallon.

And there are more or less instant sauces. One manufacturer advertises curry sauce 'with all the ingredients that you would insist on in your own kitchen-prepared sauce: wheat flour, corn-flour, tomatoes, onion and carrot powder, apples, vegetable fat, glyceryl monostereate, yeast extract, spices, flavour, sultanas, natural lemon, desiccated coconut, monosodium glutamate, caramel, edible starch, sugar, curry. salt'. I must say if I were a chef, I wouldn't insist on *all* those things but then I probably wouldn't know how to get hold of glyceryl monostereate anyway. The same firm makes a *hollandaise* sauce at 22s 6d for 6 quarts. It is, they claim 'prepared from the finest ingredients', numbered among which are those old kitchen stand-bys 'edible starch, non-fat milk solids, sodium caseinate, corn syrup solids, lecithin, hydrolyzed protein, colour and flavour'. It is, they claim 'a classic accompaniment to Grilled Salmon.'

Even in the field of natural foods, everything is being done to make life easy for the unskilled worker, of which the industry seems to attract more than its fair share. Young's, whose slogan for the trade is 'Golden profits handed to you on a plate', present a wide range of seafood products, 'all ready-coated with breadcrumbs to give a beautiful golden brown after only a few minutes frying'. Van den Bergh's offer pudding, scone, sandwich, short pastry, Yorkshire pudding and pancake mixes, 'so easy to prepare that experienced staff can use their skill in adding the attractive final touches'. Inexperienced staff just stir.

Erin foods provided a small sensation at the 1966 Hotelympia by introducing what they claimed to be, 'the first dehydrated tomato soup to taste like tomato soup. *It cooks in five minutes. Yet can be simmered for 2 to 3 hours without losing its true tomato flavour*'. Gloria Products were exhibiting their 'Blue Danube' coffee 'made to the finest standards and of such strength that you will find that three tins go as far as four of ordinary coffee'. Country Kitchen in a big notice proclaimed, 'Customers can't tell the difference between *fresh* mushrooms and Country Kitchen canned ones'. It was a theme which seemed to be repeated again and again as one walked from stand to stand. Was this the aim of food manufacturers in Britain, to reduce us to a state of mind where it was impossible to tell tinned mushrooms from fresh ones, powdered milk from cow's milk, dehydrated cabbage from real cabbage, packet soup from traditionally prepared soup, the real from the instant, the false, the fake, the substitute?

You'd have to have a very unsuspicious mind not to feel so. After all, when you can buy the ingredients of a meal of sorts for less than a shilling in packets and tins and polythene bags and paper sacks, why bother to go to such traditional places as the butcher, the greengrocer or the fishmonger for it? Most manufacturers work out for caterers their portion costs so that they can see at a glance how much per plate a dish is going to cost if they buy the ingredients so many pounds at a time. Here at random are some costs, current at the time of the 1966 Hotelympia Exhibition. All prices quoted are the most favourable you would get by bulk buying:

MANUFACTURER	PRODUCT OR RECIPE	PORTION COST
Batchelors	Apple pancakes	2·9d
	Peach and apple mallow	6·0d
	Lemon & apple meringue pie	4½d
	Apple Roly Poly	2¼d
	Apple and ginger flan	4d

B.F.G.—H

MANUFACTURER	PRODUCT OR RECIPE	PORTION COST
Symingtons	Choice of 13 soups	1·8d
	Choice of 10 jellies	6·75d (per pint)
	Complete gravy mix	3·9d (per pint)
	Original custard mix	5·29d (per pint)
	Hi-Fi instant orange juice drink	1·42d
	Mixed garden vegetables	1·76d
	Small peas	2·64d
	Blancmange powder	0·90d (per pint)
	County instant coffee	2·93d (per pint)
Carltona	Choice of 10 jellies	4¾d (per pint)
	Jelly creams	5¾d (per pint)
Swel	Tomato soup	2·19d
	Minestrone	1·67d
	Chicken	2·0d
Tea Council	Tea	0·209d– 0·369d (per cup)
McDougalls	Minestrone	2·486d
	Potage Écossais	2·258d
	Potage Espagnole	2·828d
	Potage Portugaise	2·486d
	High yield soups	1·0d
	Farm choice instant mashed potatoes	1·536d
	Melco (milk)	3¾d (per pint)

MANUFACTURER	PRODUCT OR RECIPE	PORTION COST
Cadburys	Marvel instant non-fat milk	3d (per pint)
Millac Ltd	(Reconstituted milk)	3·375d (per pint)
Wm. Moorhouse & Sons	Morning Song Hamburger	4d
California Prune Advisory Council	Prunes	1·75d

And what about the future?

At a two-day study course sponsored by the Leeds Regional Hospital Board, a hundred kitchen superintendents and senior staff heard Mr R. E. Lambert, United Leeds Hospitals Group Catering Officer, describe how, in the future, entire meals could be provided by the use of convenience foods. He gave a sample menu:

BREAKFAST

Porridge
either frozen or a mix to which only water is added

Bacon and Tomatoes
frozen or tinned

Tea or Coffee
instant product

Bread, butter, marmalade
requires no cooking

DINNER
Soup
just add water to mix

Roast beef, Yorkshire pudding
frozen or Accelerated Freeze-Dried

99

Sprouts
frozen

Mashed potato
dehydrated

Sponge pudding
from a mix

Custard
from a powder

TEA

Frozen fish and frozen crinkly chips

Vegetable
tinned, frozen or dehydrated

Sweet
egg custard from a mix

Mr Lambert told the meeting that at a recent conference in
Sweden, it was suggested that the 'future may bring the
removal of the chef from the hospital kitchen to a plant
where he would do nothing but prepare and pack
convenience foods.'
Eating in Britain it may seem that many restaurateurs have
already taken the tip and moved lock, stock and barrel into
the convenience age. At Hotelympia I tasted a mouthful of
vegetable soup, made from a large bag of powder for just over
a penny a portion. The taste was unmistakable and was
identical to the 2s portion of vegetable soup which I had eaten
for lunch the same day in a Kensington restaurant. The Age
of Convenience is not round the corner, it's here already.
Miles Quest, writing in January 1966 in *The Hotel and Catering
Times* revealed that Ford's, worried about rising costs, staff
shortages and quality control, were about to move into the
field of automation. They would cook the food for their many
different canteens in one central kitchen and then deep-freeze

it. At the other end all that will be needed is a fryer, a boiler and a re-heating oven. The food will be re-heated by warm-air convection ovens at the service points. There are problems, though, as Quest pointed out:

'Beef is usually roasted before carving and freezing; poultry is usually simmered in hot water before carving (this has been found to produce less shrinkage). Poultry also tends to deteriorate quicker, even below 0°F. Cured meats, however, have not yet been successfully frozen; the main difficulty so far has been to avoid rancidity. Sauces, too, offer freezing problems. With ordinary thickening agents, freezing tends to curdle gravies and sauces, so that they are unacceptable to the customer. The use of "waxy" starch as thickening agents has overcome this problem.'

Cooking food in some central depot and ferrying it daily to a chain of restaurants is nothing new – but the move to frozen meals, as opposed to frozen food, does mean that if you want something unusual, you're not going to get it.

One waiter in a suburban steakhouse discussed the problem of the individual in these terms. 'If you're happy to settle for what we've got, then it's quite good of its kind. You know, potted shrimps, rump steak, baked potato, ice-cream. But if you want anything unusual, you've had it. I had a couple in here last week, and he says in an offhand way, "I'll have some garlic on my steak". Well, I could hear the manager laughing a mile off. We've got no garlic here. The nearest thing we've got is a sort of reconstituted garlic dressing. Well, I like a bit of garlic on my steak too, but most people don't so you only get here what most people want.'

What is the case for convenience foods? Mr A. W. Hampton, the Catering Officer of Trust Houses, told me that he considered that convenience foods were only essential, desirable and permissible when the standard of the product reached the equivalent standard of the best food that could be made by traditional means. It's obvious that not all convenience foods on the market come up to these standards. Such a definition would immediately exclude pretty well every powdered soup product, every powdered sauce mix. Where they become essential is in those establishments which, to keep their customers, have had to pare costs to the bone. For instance, a trade journal recently described a premix in these words:

'Where the pre-mix comes truly into its own as an extender, is as an easily stored alternative when time, equipment usage and labour problems are pressing. The *bouillon* mix is, in effect, an essential escape clause in the daily administrative struggle between customer needs and the productive capacity of the kitchen.'

But the Trust House executive put his finger on the weakness of convenience foods when I asked him how useful they really are:

'I think the industry has probably been slightly misguided over convenience foods – they have not achieved, in fact, what we wanted them to achieve anyway. I mean, what some people thought they would achieve was startling economies. People are now beginning to realize that you can't save half a man and that, unless you can take your convenience food to such a pitch that you can save a whole man instead of just increasing his smoking time, then there's not much in it. I will not accept convenience foods that are inferior to those you can make yourself . . . in certain instances we compromise, but one compromises because the public very often want a compromise. Some people happen to like mayonnaise out of a bottle, or prefer tinned pineapples to fresh pineapple. If you present them with salmon mayonnaise and it tastes different from the way they have it at home, they don't like it.'

Convenience foods have already produced several generations who, like our present Prime Minister, do actively prefer tinned 'cohoe' salmon to fresh Atlantic salmon, and whose preference for convenience foods overrides economic considerations. If fresh salmon were cheaper than tinned salmon, many people would still prefer their salmon from a tin. The only coffee that the vast majority of people in Britain know how to prepare is coffee extract and instant coffee, both convenience foods. Coffee is something you spoon into a half cup of hot water to which you add milk. Of all the coffee consumed annually in Britain, instant coffee alone accounts for three-quarters – it's a market worth £35 million a year. When Nestlé's launched their new Gold Blend instant coffee, made by accelerated freeze-drying in 1965, they spent an estimated £44,000 in three weeks on nine 60-second peak hour television spots in the London area, and on Press advertising. With that sort of powerful persuasion, it's small wonder the British still make coffee by the spoonful out of a tin or bottle. As one trade writer observed recently 'there is a great fresh *v* frozen *v* air dried *v* dehydrated battle now raging among food manufacturers'. There are those like Mr Donald McLaren, Catering Manager of Goodhews who have gone on record in favour of dehydrated food. 'These are my particular fetish. I think they will eventually oust refrigerated foods. Take prawn cocktail: with frozen prawns you have to defrost a 1lb. pack. They have a limited life; if you don't get at least one order, they are wasted. Dehydrated foods need no special equipment and can be reconstituted portion by portion in a matter of seconds.'

Convenience foods have ceased to be an adjunct to good catering. That simple stage is long since past. We have arrived at the ultimate rationalization of convenience food – the entire meal prepared in the factory.

If you still think that centralized cookery is only for factories and hospitals, let me introduce you to the very latest thing in Britain – Gingham Kitchens, who are the eager bringers of 'today's fastest and most modern method of food preparation'. Already 30,000 catering operators in America are cooking the new way.

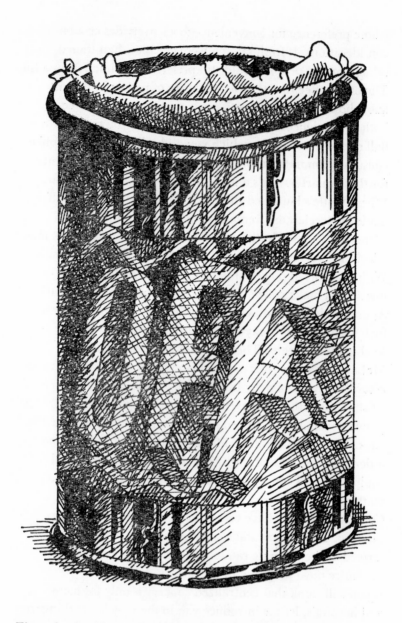

First, the food is pre-cooked and then 'blast-frozen'. In
70 seconds this food can be re-heated in a special microwave
oven. There is no steam and no cooking odours. Three times a
week, if necessary, frozen pre-cooked Gingham food is rushed

to the point of sale. You pop it into your deep freeze and, when required, microwave it into almost instant eatability, 'piping hot and succulent'.

A national image is being created in Britain giving national recognition. There are printed menus, and napkins and livery for staff. 'Everything from plates to cutlery is disposable, no fume extraction is required, and water and waste facilities need be no more than would be found in a caravan . . . with a total staff of two, 40 customers can be served with a complete meal in 15 minutes WITH NO PRIOR PREPARATION,' apart, perhaps, from taking off your hat and coat.

And what sort of food can you get? Well, so far they haven't got around to producing any British national dishes but all the food is prepared by 'Master Chefs . . using the highest quality materials and their years of skill'. If you wait 7 seconds, you can have the Big G Hot Doughnut with Whipped Cream, or in 20 seconds they can microwave up a Big G Hot Cheeseburger. You could have a 'Platter Entree' say, Bar B-Q Sausages, Creamed Potatoes and Onions in 70 seconds and, if you could only bear to wait for another 20 seconds, you could follow it with Stateside Gingham Pancakes, Maple Syrup and Lemon.

I can't wait until they start cooking the Big G Toad in the Hole with Saratoga Chips to be complemented with the Big G Devonside Baked Jam Roll with Whipped Custard.

On being done

'You must remember that the greatest psychologists of human nature are catering workers. They size up a situation and take advantage of it, or not, as the case may be. Not all catering workers are crooked, but a lot of them are bent – a bent person will take it from someone who can afford it, a crooked person will take it from anybody.'

A hotelier

This chapter is not to be taken as a wholesale condemnation of every hotel and restaurant worker in Britain. But there's no disguising the facts. The incidence of dishonesty in the catering industry is unusually high. One man, who'd been in the business all his life, explained it in this way:

'You have all that food and drink lying about. It's a terrible temptation to any man. The customers are so ignorant and apathetic that they're just crying to be done. And, let's face it, this is an industry which can't be too choosy about its employees and you get a lot of riff-raff and downright bums who'd steal the last halfpenny from their own grandma.'

William Gay, Chief Constable of British Transport Police, was quite categoric about criminality in the industry. When I went to see him to find out more about the rackets worked in the railway dining cars, he came out with a remarkable assertion, 'During the summer months, from June onwards, I reckon that in most hotels and restaurants *10 to 15 percent of the additional staff hired have criminal records.*' It is an industry where the official rewards are often so meagre, the work so unattractive, that employers are not in a position to pick and choose.

Every trade has its tricks, every job its perks. What follows are a few examples of some of the more widely practised frauds that you might find yourself unwittingly involved in. Not all of them are aimed at you, the customer. Many of them are frauds perpetrated by the employee upon his employer. In Britain most people are prepared to pay so little for their food that the possibility of cheating them is small. In the popular priced restaurants serving a three course lunch costing a few shillings, the customer almost always gets value for money. As one waiter told me 'you may get a cup of coffee put on the bill you didn't have, but most of the fiddling, if any, is by the staff against the management.'

But any catering student knows that, if you want to, it is possible to substitute something cheap for something expensive. Take fish: Ling can be substituted for cod, crayfish for lobster, whiting for haddock, plaice for sole, brill or mock halibut for halibut, Norwegian frozen salmon for fresh Scotch salmon.

But food is a minor field for profit. The great and classic fiddles occur when it comes to drink, and especially when large quantities of people are present. 'Of all branches of catering,' a hotelier told me, 'banqueting produces the biggest and best fiddles.'

The basic ploy is always to allow the client, or the organizer of the function, to order more drink than the guests will actually consume. Let me show you how it's done, or better still, let someone who's been responsible for organizing banquets for a great number of years, tell you. As he's still an active caterer, he prefers not to be named:

'Let's take a house that has a banqueting suite – a large room and a small one. Its source of business is, say, civic functions, masonics, cricket clubs, military associations, Old Boys dinners and so on. A good place should be able to do four or five functions a week in the winter, and two or three in the summer. Well, we'll say there's this big function coming off. The banqueting manager will interview a committee of the organizers over a few drinks and they'll thrash out what is usually a five course menu. It's for 250 people. The manager will work out what he can give them, bearing in mind that he'll want a 66% gross profit. There'll be absolutely no fiddling on the food, none whatever – the profit will be on the drink. Now, say the price for the ticket is forty-five bob. The breakdown will be roughly a pound for food, five or six bob for use of the room, flowers, three piece orchestra perhaps, and extras like cigarettes on the table. Printing and stationery say about sixpence a head. Perhaps, towards the end of the evening, there'll be hot soup, say 9d a head, so they're left with about 17s 6d out of your 45s. There'll be invited guests who won't pay and one or two odds and ends, but in the end they're left with about 10 to 12 shillings to have wine with. Now, a lot of these banquets don't have the best French wine. They have either the cheapest French wine or not very good Spanish wine, and most of the palate today is for Spanish white wine. Now they say 'we want $2\frac{1}{2}$ glasses of wine per person'. That means one bottle for two people, and the average price for this is about 14s so that's 7s a head. Then they'll want a sherry before dinner at 2s 6d a glass and a liqueur afterwards at 4s. Say 13s 6d, that's about £160. Now, from the point of view of the banqueting manager, he will not have given more than £100 worth of drink. You see, at a function where there are an equal number of men and women, most women have only one glass, and bent wine waiters, under the supervision of a bent banqueting manager, will only two-thirds fill a 5 ounce glass whereas a decent banqueting house would have a $6\frac{1}{2}$ ounce glass. Filling a 5 ounce glass they get 7 glasses per bottle. Filling a $6\frac{1}{2}$-ounce glass they would get only five. Depending on how well the wine waiters are trained, if there are supposed to be 125 bottles provided, the guests will go away completely satisfied with less than 100 bottles if it's properly distributed.'

You can see what is happening? Not everyone will have a liqueur, so there will be some clear profit there. At least 25 bottles of wine will not even have been opened so there's a clear profit there too. Already there will have been some remarkable saving on the pre-dinner drinks. You will remember that 2s 6d per head was laid aside for sherry. By using smaller sherry glasses than would normally be used in a hotel bar and by providing Cyprus or South African sherry, the sherry reception can become what one labourer in the banqueting vineyard described to me as 'a gilt-edged fiddle'. I asked him where the money fiddled on a banquet might go:

'The joint fiddle on the sherry, the wines and the liqueur is the perk either of the proprietor, the banqueting manager or the head wine waiter – it depends on the premises. Most banqueting fiddles do *not* go to the proprietor. They go to the banqueting manager. I know two banqueting managers whom I meet every time I go to Sandown races, and I never miss Sandown – and they're always there in the afternoon in very high-powered cars.'

Another interesting possibility when it comes to perks is the dinner, and there are many of these where drinks are paid for by the individual diners. A wine waiter told me of an incident which reveals more the stupidity of the guests than the dishonesty of the staff. There had been a dinner where the tables were arranged in the shape of an E. The chairman, who sat in the middle of the High Table, beckoned a waiter and ordered a liqueur for all the 60 guests on his table or 'sprig'. Almost simultaneously another guest, lower down, had called another waiter and ordered liqueurs for the 30 people on his side of the table. A third guest, unaware that the chairman had ordered liqueurs for the whole sprig, repeated the order to the waiter who had originally taken the chairman's order. There was so much confusion that it wasn't until the two waiters checked up in the bar later on that they found they had, in fact, served sixty liqueurs to that sprig and received payment for 150. They were, therefore, somewhat surprisingly, and gratifyingly, 90 drinks ahead at 4s each! They split the £18 two ways and marvelled at their luck.

There are also lucrative prospects after a dinner when the guests retire to another room perhaps for dancing. A waiter, who has assisted at these functions, described to me how the evening goes:

'Usually a tariff is put on the table with the price of the drinks. Say you have four or five tables. Now, the funny thing is that the rounds never come to the same price – the girls especially will often change their drinks, so it's always a different price. You pay for the drinks out of your own personal float, and you can reckon on putting another 10% on the price when you get back to the table – say it's 18s 9d, charge them £1 2s 3d. Well, on top of that whoever's paying will give you a tip, so you can make 20% per order. At the beginning, some people buy a bottle – they never put the price of a bottle on the tariff, so you can usually put quite a bit on. Most people are so taken aback at the exorbitant price that another pound doesn't make much difference. From when the meal finishes at nine until about one in the morning, you can make easily £3 or £4. Then you get paid £2 or £2 10 for your work, so that's £6 or £7 in a night, all tax-free, always tax-free.'

In outside catering, the fiddles stem from the brief which the caterer gets from the customer. Let's say that your daughter is going to get married in July, and as you're rather well-off and have a large garden at your Surrey home, you thought you might like to have it in one of those tent things; cold chicken and strawberries and some decent hock and by the time all the lists are drawn up, about two hundred people, and let's hope, for God's sake, they don't ruin the lawn.

Somebody at the Club gave you the name of some very reliable people ('They put up an absolutely first class show, old chap. Of course I don't know what it cost as I wasn't footing the bill, but give them a ring. I'm sure they're the people you want').

So you ring up and there's a meeting and, after a bit of talking round the subject, you see the size of the project and you say say 'well, as it's going to be lunch, could you do something for about a pound a head and say another pound a head for drinks.' But there are certain things you don't know.

For instance, the food cost to the caterer must be no more than 6s if he's going to make a profit. The overheads are high, carting all the equipment, breakages, special problems. He is probably operating on a gross profit margin of 66%, that is, if it costs a shilling, he must sell it for three shillings. The average wage bill is about 20%, so a normal busy organization will be showing a profit of 12%. How is the caterer going to fiddle you?

What you don't realize is that if all your guests drank a

pound's worth of booze, they'd have to be carried home. At any function, by the law of averages, there'll be 10% teetotallers and another 20% who drink very sparingly. So you're left with 70% who have about 30s. worth of booze to get through, plus all that food, plus those interminable speeches and reading of telegrams.

Supposing the caterer has convinced you that iced hock is just the drink for a summer wedding lunch, which won't be difficult, when you've heard how much a continuous flow of champagne would cost. You get five glasses out of the bottle. The caterer suggests that half a bottle per person would be reasonable. In practice, he will serve about 1½ glasses per head. To ensure that his own staff don't fiddle him, instead of sending to the function a hundred bottles, he will only send 75 – so straight away there are 25 bottles of hock which can be put on the bill and won't be argued about. In other words, even before he's got the marquee in the lorry, he's 25 bottles of hock to the good. The caterer knows right from the start that not everybody is going to turn up anyway and, even if they do, they're not going to come anywhere near drinking a hundred bottles of wine.

The fiddle on food is again a quantitive one, as an outside caterer told me:

'It's not quite like fiddling on drinks. If it's a dry outside job, in other words no drink, the quote that the catering manager will give will be very high. But if there is drink attached, then he will offset the fiddle on drink to keep the price of the food within a layman's terms of reasonableness. A layman would not understand that to produce, say, two chicken vol-au-vents, a salmon pâte, sardines on toast, plus fruit salad and ice-cream, plus tea or coffee, would mean that the caterer would have to charge an economic price of 15s. Very few laymen do appreciate the expense of outside catering, so the fiddle is invariably on the numbers – more often than not, the numbers paid for do not arrive. If a catering manager is told 300 people are coming, he will get up enough food for 250. But in the back of his organization he will have some convenience food that he can quickly prepare in case the unexpected happens. That's most unlikely, so right at the outset he has fifty covers which have been paid for and which he hasn't supplied. And that's clear profit!'

From my investigations, it doesn't seem a common practice to adulterate the drinks. If you order a cheap German wine for a dinner, you'll probably get it. But it is not unknown to bring a cheap German wine to the table in an ice-bucket with the label washed off. Floating amid the ice there might be a label from the more expensive bottle you *did* order and which you will pay for. It is not unknown for cheap Spanish wine to be bottled by a banqueting manager in perhaps Entre-Deux-Mers bottles, but when one can make money so easily in less laborious ways, it would seem an elaborate rigmarole to adopt. Nevertheless it is done. A tip of the iceberg broke surface in October 1964 when it was revealed that a leading London hotel was holding an enquiry into allegations that wine waiters had been on the fiddle. A wine butler at the hotel told *The People*:

'I think the management should know how they, and their customers, are being tricked. When I was working, my pay was £2 a night. But by fiddling to keep my job I have been averaging £20.'

He claimed the fiddle took three forms. A number of wine butlers were bringing in their own brandy at 28s a half bottle and selling it at 4s 6d a measure, which gave them a profit of £2 4s a bottle. Other waiters were filling empty wine bottles with slops from discarded glasses and serving the mixture up again. Some wine butlers were making as much as £20 a night by pouring cheap Yugoslav Riesling into bottles used for expensive hock, and selling it at 32s 6d. The chairman of the hotel company concerned was reported as saying:

'There is not a hotel or restaurant in the country that does not suffer from this sort of suggestion at some time or other . . . but you never know what goes on behind the scenes.'

I went to see a representative of the hotel allegedly involved who told me that he had interviewed all the staff and had been able to find no evidence that such an elaborate fiddle was being practised. He thought it most unlikely that the sort of people who used the hotel would be unable to distinguish between an expensive German hock and a cheap Yugoslavian one and, as for re-serving slops, he felt it impossible that this sort of thing would be done by anyone in the hotel. At another West End hotel the manager was under no illusions about his staff:

'We know that at the moment in this hotel there's a fiddle going on with the breakfasts. A fiddle whereby the waiter makes four breakfasts do for six people and pockets the profit himself. You take tonight. Say there's a dinner party of ten. Well, there's nothing to prevent the waiter charging for an extra couple of bottles of wine that haven't been consumed. Short of the host collecting the empties one by one and stacking them by his chair, how on earth can he tell how many bottles have been opened and poured? Of course they do it, bus conductors are on the fiddle. What makes you think the hotel industry's any exception?'

And yet the official view of the industry is that these practices are grossly exaggerated, even though every worker in the industry who is prepared to talk not only is able to tell you in some detail about the fiddles and how they work, but is sometimes prepared to admit he's on the fiddle himself. An ex-public schoolboy, now a sous-chef in a London hotel, told me how he'd recently been to a party in a Cambridge hotel where all the wine for a party of ten had been fiddled from a buffet supper the night before. A graduate described the complicated deception with the cakes which the staff practised on the management of an Oxbridge hotel. It seems that when

it comes to food and drink, morality is likely to fly out of
the pantry window. In the waiter's jungle, the Big Cash
Prizes go to those who are most fly, those who can conjure
two teas out of one, or four breakfasts out of two.

Every bent, or crooked, waiter has his own variations on the
old stock tricks. Substitution can be practised on a large
or small scale. For instance, there is a restaurant and bar in
London which has a dazzling display of whisky – Johnny
Walker, Teacher's, Bells, Vat 69, J & B, all the necessities a
Scotsman might require. And yet significantly large quantities
of a very cheap whisky called, for the sake of argument,
Hielan' Trash, are delivered to the cellars every week.
Hielan' Trash is not openly on display. Ask a publican how
many whisky drinkers could, if put to the test, tell the
difference between, say, a really good whisky and Hielan'
Trash, and he'll tell you that in London you could count
them on the fingers of one hand!

A barman revealed another way in which his more
unscrupulous colleagues might put a few coppers in their
pocket:

'Say you ordered a 4s 6d Scotch and he gave you a 2s 6d one.
Well then he's 2s up on his stocks. Say he does this with
different customers a dozen times – then he's 24s up on his
stocks. Now, they're pretty skilled at this, so he'll keep a mental
tally in his head as to how much he's up. When he gets an
order that comes to say, 26s, he'll ring up 2s and put the
24s in his pocket. That's an old favourite, that one.'

As you can see, the ordinary individual customer is not bilked
of very much. If he's served South African brandy for
Courvoisier at a West End hotel, he is being done, but we've
no evidence that in the really reputable hotels or restaurants
this is common practice. Most of the fiddling seems to be done
at the expense of the management, which may be why industry
leaders complain that 'overheads' are so high. And in
banqueting and outside catering, the fiddle, if engaged in, is

116

usually at the expense of a large body of people none of whom are really in a position to know whether they are being gyped or not. The really classic example of the undetectable fiddle, which the man who eventually pays the bill cannot possibly question, is the big Trade Show. It was explained to me like this:

'Let's say a plastics firm have made an industrial film, you know, one of those things in colour saying how marvellous the product is. Well, before and after the showing there's an open bar. Say at this Trade reception there's 500 guests, drinks with cheese straws and olives and peanuts. There are 4 or 5 white-jacketed barmen plus 7 or 8 waiters or waitresses. Well, after the film all these people dash to the bar and start ordering free drinks for each other. Instead of having a beer, which they probably would do if they were buying it themselves, they start ordering brandy and what have you. Now the client will hear people ordering whiskies and

brandies and gins galore, and he'll get slightly alarmed but
he'll probably say well, it's a business expense, and that's
that. But if all those people walk out under their own steam,
which they will, they could not physically have consumed
at the most more than 15s worth of drink – 15s is a lot of
money even at cocktail bar prices. The fiddle is that the
organizer gets a bill that works out at 30s a head, sometimes
£2.'

I asked my informant what happened to the overcharge
which, on his reckoning, might at one of these affairs be as
much as £200:

'Whoever is working the fiddle will have a special part of his
cellar where the man who checks the weekly stock never goes.
So in the West End a man, doing a lot of these Trade Shows,
may have a thousand pounds worth of stock that has already
been paid for many times over by different organizers. How
does he convert this illegal float of drink into cash? Well,
he waits for another kind of function, one where people are
paying cash for their drinks. At the end of the do, instead of
ringing up all the money in the till, they extract a proportion
of it and make up the diminished stocks of drink from their
own illegal float. So the bar, instead of having taken £200,
might only take £110. The other £90 is the fiddle.'

Although a high percentage of fiddles are staff *v* management
fixtures, there are the staff *v* customers *v* management where
you get gyped as well.
An unrewarding staff *v* customers match where the staff
won hands down occurred in a large West End Hotel not so
long ago. The occasion was a reception to celebrate a
Commonwealth country's National Day. I was there for
forty minutes and failed to get within stretching distance of a
drink. I put it down to meanness on the part of my hosts, that
or lack of organization. I found out afterwards that crates and
crates of diplomatic drink had been sent to the hotel, more

than enough for every guest, even if each one had been an alcoholic. Long before the function began, large quantities of champagne, sherry, gin and whisky disappeared. There was no redress from the hotel because the management were totally unaware and innocent of any fraud being operated. There is no doubt, however, in the minds of the High Commission concerned that a large quantity of their drink went out by the back door.

An example of the fiddle, whereby the customer pays for something he doesn't get, has been worked on and off for years on railway trains and, to a lesser extent (because there are fewer of them), on cross-channel ferries.

If you've ever eaten in a restaurant car and thought the portions strangely small, there's a possibility that the staff were eking out the supplies to provide extra meals. The money for these extra meals is shared between them. The staff are required to give a receipt for each meal taken, but by using old bills left in the dining car, or slipping the carbon paper out of the bill book so that no trace of the bill they hand out remains, large sums of money can be swindled annually.

It's not possible to find out how wide-spread the fiddling is, but William Gay of the British Transport Police told me that the prosecutions represent a very small proportion of the cases of swindling that take place. If you take three years at random, you'll find that in 1960 there were 31 prosecutions involving, among other crack-trains the Talisman, the Brighton Belle and the Northumbrian. In 1961 there were 24 prosecutions involving the Talisman, the Cornish Riviera, the Red Dragon, the Master Cutler, the Torbay Express and the Pines Express. In 1964 some of the named trains involved in the 13 prosecutions were the unlucky Talisman, the West Riding, the Royal Duchy and the White Rose.

In 1965 there was a successful prosecution of the chief cashier and seven stewards on the cross-channel ferry Maid of Orleans. Here it wasn't so much the customers that were being fiddled as the till. After one of these successful

prosecutions which, incidentally, cost British Rail
thousands of pounds and many patient hours of enquiry,
the receipts always rise spectacularly. If we take one case,
you'll see how a typical swindle is worked.

In the early 1950's passengers on the 7.15 a.m. Harwich to
Liverpool Street train, known as The Hook of Holland,
began to complain about the minute portions they were
served for breakfast: a scrap of scrambled egg, a small bit of
bacon, a tiny sausage. Letters of complaint about these
pigmy meals were received by *The Times*, the *Amsterdam
Telegraaf* and also by the Hotels Executive.

After this had been going on for some time, the wheels were
put in motion. Sixteen plain-clothes police officers, men and
women, kept watch on what happened on board the Hook of
Holland as it sped towards London. When they had assembled
their evidence, the case came up at the Old Bailey. It turned
out that on three particular mornings they had observed
108, 40 and 73 breakfasts being served. When the returns
were examined, the number had shrunk to 81, 34 and 49.
The fiddle was simple because each bill was the same – 4s.
Every time a used bill was re-issued to another passenger,
the extra 4s was divided among the staff of the dining-car.
All of them were in the racket, some enthusiastically, some
with misgiving. After the Common Sergeant had weighed
them off for a total of 12 years and 8 months behind bars,
receipts bucked up on the Hook of Holland. An increase of
64 breakfasts was recorded in the following week. When you
realize that on this one train, just serving breakfasts, the 5-man
dining car crew were making between them £624 a year
tax-free, over and above their wages and their tips, you'll
realise the size of the potential loss British Rail is
exposed to.

Very few people in the industry know the answer to the
problem of fiddling. At one time it was thought that portion
control – the system of doling out so much food per person –
might cut down losses, but portion control is an integral

part of the dining-car system and swindling still goes on. Some of the frauds are so ingenious that a normal person wouldn't think them feasible. A former lecturer at a technical college told me:

'Students I taught used to come back and tell me of fiddles I would never conceive of. Like dipping the rim of a glass in a saucer of gin, adding ice and orange squash and serving it as gin and orange.'

I asked Michael Nightingale of the Hotel and Catering Institute why there was so much fiddling, and he suggested that basically it existed because there wasn't a proper structure of supervision. 'In other words, your departmental heads are not completely for the management. Because there's lack of supervision, the temptations come in. If you had good supervision in the first place, the temptation wouldn't have been there.'

Sometimes the supervision itself can be bent. And when the pressures to join in a fiddle are strong, it is sometimes impossible to resist, especially if it means losing one's job as well. A man who now holds a responsible post in the training side of the industry told me just how strong the pressures can be:

'I was in a job where a new manager was appointed. I was responsible for the liquor stocks directly to the accountant for percentages and so on. This manager approached me before one function and asked me to exchange some empty bottles of spirits for full ones. Well, I knew what he was up to. He was going to supply less drink than would be paid for. I told him I wasn't prepared to do this. One, I didn't think it was right, and two, I'd been involved in taking the booking for this function. They'd been coming to the hotel for years – I knew them, and I reckon you build up business on mutual understanding and service and so on, and I said "No". I got fired the following day for something else, but I knew why I got fired – and so did the manager.'

With strong pressure on the one side and the almost incredible naïvety of the British consuming public on the other, it's small wonder that fiddling is so widespread. Perhaps the strangest thing about the classic Case Of The Missing Breakfasts on the Harwich run is that even when the dining-car crew started serving powdered *soup* with breakfast to eke out the rations, nobody thought it strange.

Blame the workers in the industry if you like, but surely our own pathological dislike of complaining, however unusual or suspicious the circumstances, is in its way not only a positive incitement to villainy, but also a form of passive connivance.

Amid the waving palms

'Tipping should be treated as corruption and bribery, which in many cases it is.'

Vernon Duker, Vice-Chairman of Torquay Hotels Association – September, 1965.

On the 17th July, 1961, a former cloakroom attendant at a leading London hotel stood up in the High Court and alleged that he had worked at the hotel for 20 years without getting any wages. He told Mr Justice Sachs that he was given a uniform, free meals and a share of the *tronc*. He claimed that in a bad summer, he got as little as £3 or £4 a week, but in other weeks it went up to £13. He'd begun working there for nothing in 1931. The hotel denied employing him since 1948 when they had appointed a concessionaire to run the cloakroom.

I once said to a hotel manager: 'There's a man in your lavatory with a begging bowl. He seems to be doing rather well. It's full of florins and half-crowns' 'Begging bowl, sir?' 'Yes, a quite well-dressed, well-spoken man, handing people towels, and he's got this begging bowl beside him.' 'I think you must be mistaken, sir. He's certainly not begging.' But that's what it seemed like to me. Perhaps I wasn't feeling in a good mood. I'd already paid two lots of half-a-crown as a cover charge to help the hotel pay for laundering my tablecloth and paper napkin and as a subscription towards the bread I'd eaten with the meal. Having spent about £4 on the meal, the waiter then added another eight shillings surcharge in order to help the hotel offer him a decent wage. When he brought the change, he hovered round the saucer smiling nervously and bowing and hoping that I was going to leave what was there.

To complete the scene, I half expected to find the receptionist touting at the door for contributions towards the cost of the plastic flower arrangements, and the manager's wife by the lift whining and selling clothes pegs. Had the manager himself appeared with a card round his neck saying 'Please give generously – only your charity can save us from ruin and the degradation of the poorhouse' I would not have been surprised. In fact, in many hotels I find it strange that the whole kitchen staff don't line up in the front hall abasing themselves for tips.

125

They don't, of course. However, the really good restaurant
or hotel does position a representative on the front steps to
wring the last penny from you. He's a great seven-foot high
linkman, gorgeously caparisoned in gold epaulettes and
medals. He, too, is living on what he can squeeze from the
parting guest. He doesn't have a bowl, just this great pink
ungloved hand waiting to be crossed with silver in return for
which, with any luck, he'll salute you and call you 'sir'.
In a country like India where there are a hundred men for
every job and famine round the corner, one is not surprised
by the number of beggars but in Britain, where there is full
employment, it seems strange that the hotel and restaurant
industry should still encourage their staff to tout for extra
cash in this embarrassing way. Many people, like myself,
see tipping as a hangover from the days when people were
inadequately paid or not paid at all. You threw a penny to
the little ragged crossing-sweeper because you knew that if
you and the other gentry didn't tip him, the poor little beggar
would starve to death – either that or he'd move to some less

marginal crossing and you'd get your boots all covered with muck. But it still seems remarkable that in the midst of plenty, grown men should vie with one another for the privilege of standing outside hotels in the rain and whistling for taxis. One of the reasons why the English don't make good waiters, I'm told, is that it's too disgustingly servile a job for people with our proud heritage. I wonder. Soliciting for sixpences in restaurant lavatories is pretty servile, and running for taxis for people in the hope of getting a reward is pretty servile . . . or is it in some specious way thought to be less degrading than bringing something to eat? Why in the welfare state do we still tip? Here are five statements I got from people in London:

'If a waiter or somebody has looked after you, then I think it's up to you to show your appreciation over and above what he gets in wages.'

'I give two shillings in the pound, never more never less, except if it's just a cup of tea then I leave sixpence.'

'As a socialist, I think tipping is all wrong, but if you don't tip, the poor devil's not going to get a living wage so what's the alternative? While they keep tipping, everybody's got to fall in line.'

'I don't like tipping. I reckon if you've paid a fair price for a meal, then they ought to be able to pay a waiter's money out of the profit, not expect you to hand over more. I think it's a racket.'

'They like to be tipped, and it's all income tax free, don't forget that. They'd rather get it that way than legally in their wages. That's what they come flocking over here for – tax-free tips!'

For nearly everyone on the giving end, tipping is a source of great embarrassment. If often turns a pleasant relationship into one of master and servant. If you are over-lavish, you may feel that the only attitude you are generating is contempt, if you give too little you are quite often conscious of sullen dislike. If you talk to people in Britain about tipping, you find that they genuinely believe that the catering industry pays an unfair wage for the job, and that only their private charity keeps a waiter from stealing milk to feed his children. Even though on many occasions if you were to compare the basic cost of the meal with the price charged you might consider that the profit built into the price was sufficient to give the hotelier a long winter holiday in the sun and his staff a reasonable wage. On the normal restaurant mark-up for wine one has paid the cost of the service several times over – to be expected to contribute an additional levy in the form of a tip could be regarded as little short of preposterous.

The tip is no longer given for service rendered. It's become an expected part of the bill and, even if the service is inadequate, a tip is considered mandatory. So one is no longer tipping as a gesture of thanks. The tip is a surcharge – no matter how appalling the service, a £5 meal is going to cost you at least £5 10s unless you are prepared to flout convention. One might approve the principle of giving 10% for a job well done if conversely one were entitled to deduct 10% for a job not well done.

Various people in the industry have condemned tipping. A common view expressed to me was:

'The ultimate ideal is to do away with tipping, but the staff are now conditioned to expecting tips. They look on this as part of their salary. Now I would like to see the tip or extra money coming in a different way, and I think we can only get this by introducing a service charge. This would encourage people to stop tipping. It would then be up to the company to distribute the 10% service charge fairly. The next step would be to put prices up by 10% and abolish the service charge – then if I were a hotelier I might consider giving my staff a sort of sales bonus – there would be an incentive to give good service, but the customer wouldn't be expected to tip.'

The service charge was almost completely unknown in Britain before the war. But in recent years there has been a rationalizing move towards the certainty of the service charge as opposed to the unpredictability of voluntary tipping. In 1962 Trust Houses introduced a 10% service charge in its 200 or so hotels. Not all hotels have followed this lead. British Rail have a voluntary system – they'll put a service charge on the bill if you find that easier than dispensing individual tips.

As an outsider, I cannot see that a service charge is anything other than an additional increase in the charge for food and drink and accommodation. For instance, if a couple went to a hotel and reckoned on spending a fortnight and the terms were, say, 20 guineas a week, they might reasonably expect a bill of, say, £84, that is if they didn't have any extras like early morning tea, or supplementary dishes and they had nothing to drink. That would be their minimum bill. But, with a service charge, they would be asked to pay an additional £8 8s. If they did have any extras, this additional charge might well be £10. It's not every middle-class family man, after a fortnight at the seaside, having costed his holiday perhaps to the last pound, who would normally rush round in a fit of generosity distributing a tenner to the staff. But this is what a service charge compels him to do. As someone, who found himself in this position, expressed it:

'In my case I found that I had a bill of £138 for the fortnight. We'd had one or two relations in the town in for a meal and, of course, there'd been the odd bottle of wine. Well, I felt I'd been a good customer of the hotel. We'd used the bar well, we're a big family and I'd always bought the barman a drink. In a small way we'd brought people into the hotel who wouldn't normally have come – I had no complaint about the food or the rooms or anything. The service was the usual sort of holiday thing, a lot of students trying to be helpful and it was all a bit amateurish, but then when I got the bill on the morning I left, there was this additional charge of nearly £14. Well, nobody in his right mind would dish out fourteen quid's worth of tips, not unless he was the Aga Khan. But there it was in black and white. If I had been tipping myself, I might have given four or five quid to the very few members of the staff who really had gone out of their way to give service – after all, that's what a tip's for, service! But £14, well I'm never going to be had that way again.'

What is not generally recognized is that an increasingly large part of any hotel bill is composed of various forms of taxes. Beer, wines, spirits and cigarettes all contain a high proportion of tax. To be asked to pay an additional ten or fifteen per cent as a 'service charge' on goods which are already highly taxed is both illogical and unnecessary. The hotel and catering industry estimates that the new employment tax will cost it £30 million a year. This tax will be reflected in the higher prices charged by the industry. Do they intend to impose an additional 'service charge' on the tax charge? It seems they will. The public will no doubt pay without a quibble. Again, in most hotels and restaurants a service charge is fairly distributed, but this is not always the case. In February, 1966 *The Caterer and Hotelkeeper* published a letter under the heading, 'Wanted: a square deal for genuine hotel staff.'

'How many hoteliers can honestly say that they give their staff really good food and accommodation? How many keep promises made to staff on engagement, especially at seasonal hotels?'

The correspondent described how she and her husband were employed as managers in a Cornish hotel and promised a share of the 10% service charge on all bills:

'My husband ran the bar the whole season with only one

evening off and no extra money and no 10%. At the end of
13 weeks, I was told that that I was no longer required . . .
My husband was told he could stay to the end of the season
if he wished. Neither of us got a penny of the 10% and none
of the kitchen staff did either. In fact, the amount that was
paid out was only about one tenth of what they had collected
off the bills. I should think that the 10% paid their wages for
the season. If my husband had wanted he could have lined
his pockets well from the bar, but we have always played the
game.'

The Caterers' Record, official journal of the National Caterers'
Federation, protested against the 'vicious circle' of service
charges and tips in 1964. An editorial suggested that in
principle tipping should be abolished: 'Today it appears
another way of soaking the public'. But their main criticism
was of the service charge which they claimed often went to
the hotelier. Their solution was to get back to the old
method whereby a waiter must give of his best – otherwise no
tip.
While the expectation of a tip remains officially recognized
by the Wages Council – hotel workers who are not likely to
be tipped get higher rates of pay – very little can be done about
outlawing this anomalous practice. Although it's not likely
we shall ever see the pre-1939 days when doormen actually
paid a hotel to be allowed to come within forelock-touch
distance of the rich, very few people in the industry see tipping
ever completely disappearing.
Tipping is certainly degrading. It also can operate unfairly.
It may happen in large hotels and restaurants where a *tronc*
is operated that some people get a great deal and some get
very little. A waiter told me how the *tronc* was doled out in a
restaurant where he was working:

'We were busy pretty well all the time and the *tronc* came to
about £250 a week. The two casual commis got £2 10s a
week each, the four commis got a fiver, two demi-chefs got

between £8 and £10, the five chefs-de-rang got £16 to £18 each, and the rest was shared out between the two head-waiters and the restaurant manager – they did all right really.'

Tipping is never going to be fair, or even square. There are always those who will pocket what is intended for others, or intercept more than their share on the way down the chain. On the face of it, the gradual elimination of tipping by a service charge, which would eventually appear as a concealed charge in the meal itself, seems reasonable but would it work? I put the theory to a hotel executive:

'It's all very well in practice. I would like to see tipping done away with. We all would, but it's here to stay. We will never get rid of tipping because there will always be greedy men, big-headed men who, for one reason or another, want to show off in front of their guests – it may be their customer, their client or even their mistress. But that person wants the people he's with to think that the staff jump for him and him alone and if that costs a fiver, he'll pay it. And if one person tips, everybody else has to fall in line.'

And yet I wonder if he's right. Tipping in one growing and important part of the catering world has been totally abolished. It seems that if you pay a man or a woman a proper wage, and thereby recognize their self-respect, and if at the same time you categorically inform the customer that tipping is forbidden, tipping withers and dies. The airlines which serve millions of meals and drinks every year have generated an atmosphere where offering a tip would be regarded as insolent and impertinent.
How long will it be before the catering industry, still grounded in the past, begins to wake up to what the public wants?

Eating out in Noshleigh

'It is regrettable that despite two reminders only 65% of the restaurants co-operated and it is hard to understand the attitude of a well-known firm of a chain of restaurants, which replied, "We have already given the information you require to several similar organizations as yourself and we feel this is sufficient," or of a proprietor who refused saying, "This is a private-enterprise restaurant".'

Extract from the preface to the Hampstead Consumer Group's report on eating out in Hampstead

According to the *Good Food Guide* large areas of Britain are almost devoid of places that can honestly be recommended for a meal. You'll drive for long hungry miles in the East Riding, Lincolnshire, Northumberland, much of Wales and Scotland before you'll get something worth eating. Even in more thickly populated areas the choice is often not between good and bad food but between bad food and not too bad food. Recent consumer reports from Oxford, Hampstead, Durham, Ipswich, Belfast, Sheffield, Cambridge, Brighton, Dartford, Croydon, Barnsley, Crawley, Watford and Carlisle make sad reading.

They may have limited value, their criteria may be wrong, but they indicate that eating out is often far from pleasurable. The reports vary from full-scale investigations in Oxford and Hampstead to more limited operations. Some of them are no doubt highly subjective – like the one compiled by the three ladies of Durham who visited fourteen establishments serving coffee and solemnly asked for one weak coffee, one strong coffee and one standard coffee. But their criticism should be read by every caterer in Britain. Comments like these take a lot of explaining away:

'The vegetables arrived lukewarm.'

'White wine was not chilled.'

'A cat and dog were allowed to enter the restaurants and permitted to roam about.'

The writer was unable to get hot milk but the assistant offered hot milk as long as she could put a dash of coffee in it as 'we are not allowed to serve the milk without something in it'.

'The waitress needs a bath.'

'I would like the soup hot' . . . 'It's just out of the oven, sir!'

'We asked whether they had fresh gorgonzola as the piece on the dish looked dry, whereupon the waiter turned it over and put it on my plate.'

135

'If you enjoy your coffee weak, we recommend —'

'Hot food was served on a cold plate and service was willing but inexpert.'

'It is surprising that 8.30 is the latest time one can order dinner at the town's leading hotel.'

'Outside privy with a door that will not close.'

'No surprise or even interest was shown when our almost untouched plates were removed.'

Consumer groups engaged in compiling these reports are not always taken seriously. In Sheffield they hopefully sent out questionnaires to be filled in by individual proprietors and they reported:

'We discounted one form which was filled in for Eric's Road Caff which he claimed was a City Hotel. Under *Licensed?* he put, "for what?" and *Any other comments?* read "Music and Dancing – I like them both". *Any other?* "I like that too." '

In Oxford a team of volunteers ate 250 meals 'ranging from the superb to the abysmal'. There are 73 restaurants in the town, of which 5 qualified for inclusion in the 1965/66 *Good Food Guide*. But, said the Oxford Consumers Group report 'mediocrity is still our main complaint . . . in many cases it is dreary fare. Oxford's many bedsitter-dwellers who have to eat out must have a monotonous diet of grills, chips and peas.' In Hampstead, the Consumer Group investigated 119 restaurants, of which 10 appeared in the current *Good Food Guide*. The report found that while in many restaurants the standard of hygiene was high, in others it was 'appalling'. They found a few places 'which serve such dreadful food to so few people that we wonder how they manage to stay open at all'. There was harsh criticism 'particularly of tasteless food, soggy potatoes, hard pastry, stale cakes and poor coffee'. I read a bunch of these consumer reports at one sitting and it had rather the same effect as eating a pack of those biscuits that make you slim – your appetite is taken away and you feel vaguely uncomfortable.

So far nobody has done a survey of a small Midland or Northern town, an omission which we hasten to rectify. Noshleigh, population 63,000, prospered in the Industrial Revolution and grew from a market town to a manufacturing centre of some regional significance. From about the turn of the century it's been in a state of decline, but most people have only just woken up to the fact. Noshleigh is still living in the Steam Age, fighting a plucky if doomed rear-guard action in the export battle. There's not so much brass about as there used to be and one or two works have had to close down. Noshleigh has lost a lot of its old secure markets in the outposts of what was once the British Empire. But management is still strictly amateur and play-it-by-ear, workers still happily caught up in a self-strangling net of restrictive practices. Noshleigh, strongly evangelical, draughty on winter nights, grimy, black-bricked, cobbled, has a small and dedicated group of consumers, this is their report:

A Guide to Noshleigh Restaurants
Compiled by the Noshleigh Consumer Group
2s 6d (postage 5d)

ACKNOWLEDGEMENT

The Committee of the Noshleigh Consumer Group wish to express their gratitude to the one restaurant manager who attempted to fill in our questionnaire.

INTRODUCTION

We defined for the purpose of our survey a restaurant as a place where you could sit down to eat, although on Market Day this was not always applicable. There are 9 such eating

establishments in and around Noshleigh of which none is as
yet listed in the *Good Food Guide*, although many of them are
advertised in the Noshleigh Chamber of Commerce almanack
and in the *Noshleigh Gazette* as well as on slides at the Plaza
cinema. Our 7 members consumed 19 meals, at their own
expense, in Noshleigh's 9 restaurants and their reports, are
set out below.

SUMMARY AND GENERAL COMMENT

Although no one would claim that Noshleigh is becoming a
gastronomic centre, nevertheless in some restaurants the food
is less tasteless than others. Members were particularly
appreciative of the warmth of many of the restaurants.
Noshleigh is notoriously windy in the long winter months, and
to get out of the cold is a treat in itself. Although many of
the restaurants under review have no toilet facilities, they are
all within easy walking or running distance of the Town Hall
Conveniences which are open until 6.30 at night. Members
were impressed by the wide choice of foods, hot and cold, and
the variety of regional dishes – which, of course, includes our
justly celebrated Noshleigh Pudding, which is, as many
gourmets testify, a meal in itself.
There was praise for the gay décor of some of our cafes,
although one or two members felt, in certain cases, the variety
of colours was perhaps too exuberant for so Northern a town.

REPORT

NOSHLEIGH TRANSPORT CAFE

Although its clientele are mainly knights of the road, (our
good friends the long distance lorry drivers) it is also
patronized by the bus-crews of the Noshleigh and District
Motor Transport Company and various young women who
seem to spend their time commuting about the country in the

cabs of lorries. The vicar's wife, who was the only member of the group to visit the Café, reported that on the Saturday afternoon that she paid her visit, it was almost impossible to hear anything. 'There was a great abundance of noise coming from a large machine with a glass front which a group of Noshleigh young folk, none of whom I recognized as being members of the St. George's Youth Club, were feeding with sixpences. There was also a constant din of accelerating motor bicycles.' The vicar's wife, who confined her sampling to a cup of tea, ('Hot, very strong and much of it in the saucer,') said that the menu was on a large blackboard, ('a very sensible arrangement,') and that the helpings seemed to be generous. She did not stay for long as she was conscious of being the object of some comment by what she took to be the regulars. When she left the café, she found both of the tyres on her bicycle were punctured and the basket missing – 'Surely too unusual to be a coincidence.'

THE STATION HOTEL

Although not strictly a restaurant, food can be obtained here at times. Members commented favourably on the sausages on stick 8d, slice of veal and ham pie with half tomato 2s 3d, pickled eggs 10d, and sandwich rounds. The landlord serves the food himself, although, on nights when there is all-in wrestling on the bar telly, he is not anxious for this kind of custom. Perhaps he tends to underestimate the demand for food as on several occasions when members called in, they found the glass display case empty. Crisps and packets of salted peanuts on a card are usually in stock.

WIN'S DINER

At the lower end of the town, this small restaurant caters for those who want a cheap filling meal in a hurry. There is a *table d'hôte* lunch (soup, joint, pudding) which members

report to be fairly good value for 2s 3d. There is usually a
thick soup to start with and plenty of veg. with the cut off the
joint. The custard is a bit thin, reported one member. On
Saturdays, Win's Diner does a very attractive high tea for
folk from the outlying areas. A sample meal at 3s 6d was
bread and butter, pot of tea, rasher and fried egg, sausage and
tinned tomato, slice of cake. Music is provided through a
loudspeaker. No licence. One member took a half bottle of
wine in, but the proprietor, when requested, supplied 4 glasses
only under protest. Our questionnaire was sent back torn up
in shreds with an illiterate and rude note which, for various
reasons, we do not print in this report.

THE CALYPSO

Despite glowing testimonials from nearly all our members,
Mr Raymond Postgate persistently refuses to include The
Calypso in his Guide. Signor Paulo, whose enterprise the
Calypso is, remains undeterred. Bookings are heavy specially
on early closing day and Saturday night and, as
more and more Noshleigh folk are getting the eating-out
habit, The Calypso is likely to remain a firm favourite. The
decorations are lively and the Italian music creates a pleasant
ambiance. Carlo, a cheerful little Londoner, specializes in a
variety of spaghetti dishes (pork chop and spaghetti 5s 6d,
liver and spaghetti 5s, Irish stew and spaghetti 4s 6d, chicken
in the basket and spaghetti 7s, spaghetti in tomato sauce 3s 6d).
Try too his delicious soups and *pâté maison*. Special dishes are
Scampi Carlo (served with spaghetti) and *escalope au riz
Carlo grande*. Chips and a vegetable are included in the price
of the main meal. There is a moderately expensive wine list,
but wine can be bought by the glass (4s 6d).

THE TAJ MAHAL

The premises have been temporarily closed by the Noshleigh
Medical Officer for Health after a lot of tummy upsets.

Mr Rajagopalachari, who runs The Taj Mahal, specializes in curry dishes which are certainly a welcome change from the routine of English food. Prawn Briani 17s 6d, Vegetable curry 17s 6d, tropical fruit salad 7s 6d, seem to be the mainstay of the menu. One member reported a large amount of gristle and bone in a plate of something which he was given, but this may have been a special Indian delicacy. Although the restaurant is mostly empty, it does add an international note to Noshleigh's eating facilities. Prices are perhaps on the high side but as the waiters have to be brought nearly 5,000 miles from their native India, overheads must be heavy. We wish Mr Rajagopalachari success in his efforts to bring The Taj Mahal up to our very high Noshleigh standards of hygiene.

THE COUNTY HOTEL

Almost entirely favourable **reports** here. Good service, wholesome food and an aura of bygone coaching elegance. It is perhaps a lengthy process waiting to be served in the somewhat chilly dining-room but the food, when it comes, is always welcome. Mrs Lovett, who does the cooking is in many ways an eccentric personality, and what she turns her hand to is often a surprise. On the occasion when one member visited The County, she had tried her hand at a baked *risotto* and, although it was a little 'chewy', it was at least an attempt to break away from her somewhat rigid pattern of mixed grill or roast. Perhaps, Mrs Lovett, this difficult sort of cooking is best left to the Signor Carlos of this world with their flair and expertise. Mrs Lovett is a cook of the old school, brought up in the days when prolonged boiling of all vegetables was considered essential to the digestive process. But there is one consolation, everything at The County is always *well-done* which is nice to know especially when one is eating pork. There is a wide selection of Empire wines. Small weddings are also undertaken. Hot dinners served until 7.30 p.m. Saturdays late extension till 8.15 p.m.

THE DINGLEY DELL

A long established and popular restaurant, The Dingley
Dell occupies a warm place in the affections of Noshleigh
people. The dainty lunches and light teas are always of the
best quality and everything is homemade, even the Noshleigh
Pudding. At 3s 6d a portion (Weds. & Sats.) the Pudding is
almost as famous as Noshleigh Stump. Made of sheep's blood,
tripe, spleen, pigs bladder, grot and trotter jelly, Noshleigh
Pudding and swedes is part of our national heritage. Frozen
Noshleigh Pudding is exported to wherever Noshleigh folk
have migrated, and the annual Noshleigh Dinner in Bombay
used to be one of the Highlights of the Colonial year.

'Noshleigh Pud and Noshleigh brain,
Conquered mountain, sea and plain.
Men on Noshleigh Pudding bred
Are strong-in-the-arm and weak in the head.'
Chas. Nibbett (1854–1912)

RAMSBOTTOM'S FISH PARLOUR

This old traditional fish restaurant in Station Road is like a
magnet on dark winter nights. Its cheery lights shine out when
all the other shops are long since closed. The grand smell of
frying and the clouds of smoke pouring out of the open door
bear witness to the dexterity of the Ramsbottom family,
father, son and grandson, in the gentle art of frying. The
familiar FRYING TONITE whitewashed on the window
draws large crowds from all walks of life. Since the
Ramsbottoms moved out to the new estate, their back parlour
and upstairs living accommodation has furnished three rooms
where food can be consumed on the premises. The menu is a
simple one: fish, chips and tinned marrowfat peas. Prices are
moderate, and salt and vinegar *ad lib*. Various tasty
proprietary drinks are on sale. The Ramsbottoms have
discontinued a new line which they introduced last summer

'Chicken-'n'-Chips'. As facilities were limited, the frozen chicken pieces had to be fried in the same fat as the fish, and customers commented unfavourably on the experiment.

An evening out at Ramsbottom's can cost as little as 2s 9d although most folk go overboard for additional portions of chips. The main parlour is illuminated with winking Christmas lights all the year round. Closed Sundays and Christmas Day.

THE PLAZA CINEMA TUDOR CAFE

A favourite gathering place for Noshleigh young folk, the Tudor Cafe provides not only a pleasant rendezvous for afternoon teas, morning coffee or a cooling ice on warm days, but also does attractive lunches and snack suppers. The room is tastefully decorated with imitation Tudor plasterwork and 'wooden beams' and hung with coloured photographs of such famous film stars as Jessie Matthews, George Arliss, W. C. Fields, Jean Harlow and other mighties of the silver screen. The lunches at 3s 9d are really good value. A sample menu consisted of a good thick soup, Country Pie (minced meat and vegetables in a pastry case) sprouts, boiled potatoes and a choice of ice-cream or Bakewell tart and custard to follow. A new innovation at the Plaza is the hot dog stand in the foyer. The hotdogs (a sausage placed in a partially sliced open bridge roll) are a good buy at 1s 6d and their pleasing aroma provides a novel welcome on cold nights. As the Plaza is shortly to be converted into a supermarket perhaps this information is slightly irrelevant but the Tudor Cafe has so long been a part of the Noshleigh scene that we cannot see it depart without a mention in this report.

Lead kindly guide

'Nor do we accept the two main defences of the caterer against the guides. The first is that chance visits are unfair because it is possible that the chef or some other essential member of the staff has his day off. This is a fallacious argument. Following this to its logical conclusion, it means that a restaurant open seven days a week is likely to offer a poor meal for over 28% of the time it is open, if the chef is off for two days a week . . . Nor do we subscribe to the view that only expert caterers can adequately judge the value of food. This has the air of caterers trying desperately to preserve the aura of their own mystique.'

Leader in The Hotel and Catering Times 6*th January*, 1966

'The *Guide* shines like a small honest light in a great gastronomic darkness.'

Member of the Good Food Club

The local consumer reports on eating out have been influenced almost entirely by one man and one book. The man is Raymond Postgate, the Savonarola of British Cuisine, founder and President of the Good Food Club, launched in 1949 under the title 'The Society for the Prevention of Cruelty to Food'. The Book – the 800-page *Good Food Guide*. The members of the Club are the thousands of men and women who buy the *Guide*, which since 1962 has been organized and financed by the Consumers' Association. It is sixteen years since the first *Guide* appeared; today there are about 13,000 members who religiously fill out their report cards. There are 160 connoisseurs who check on the 13,000 reporting members and a small paid staff who check on the 200 connoisseurs. The Club has undoubtedly done more than any other single organization to raise the standard of restaurant and hotel food in Britain. There is a constant nagging by the Founder and his members against bottled mayonnaise, packet soup, stringy over-cooked meat in tiny portions, pretentiousness, sodden vegetables, tinned fruit with packet custard, synthetic coffee, *pâté maison* out of a tin, over-charging for wine, farcical *flambé* cooking, noisy canned music, luke-warm food, dirty crockery and cutlery.

Today *The Good Food Guide* is weighty and financially successful. Its last edition sold over 100,000 copies. For the good restaurant, inclusion in the *Guide* can mean the difference between failure and success. Just before this book was published I went to the *Guide* headquarters to talk to their chief inspector. He is in the full bloom of middle-age, wise in wine and food-ways, and because he spends his working life travelling round Britain checking on reports, he wishes to remain unnamed. Here are some of the questions I put to him, and his answers:

What kind of people send in reports?
Our membership has vastly increased since the Consumers' Association bought up the *Guide*, we got a lot of *Which?*

readers for the first time, so that now quite a few of the fantastic number of reports are from people who don't know a great deal about food but are learning.

What are the most common complaints you receive?
People complain about service and reception, the atmosphere, delays in bringing dishes, forgetting to offer wine until the main course is over. Oddly enough they rarely complain of dirtiness, which I find interesting because I certainly see enough of it. Small helpings are complained of, and the tastelessness of so much of the food.

What do your members dislike the most about eating out?
I think pretentiousness, they dislike that intensely. I think that's a Raymond Postgate characteristic which is passed on to his members. We have a glorious story of one of our inspectors going to a restaurant which was doing extremely well up in the North but which was inclined to be a bit pretentious and which had put on the menu, 'The chef would be delighted to cook any dish you like'. Our inspector thought for a bit and then asked for a steak *Tartare*, and was astonished when the waiter said to him, 'How would you like it done?' He said he'd like it raw, and the waiter pulled himself together and went off. Eventually he was, in fact, served a medium-done steak. I noticed on the bill which he attached to his report the dish was recorded as 'Steak Tata'.

Is there a move towards cooking complicated dishes badly?
Well, there's a great increase in cooking things like duck *à l'orange*, but badly. I've got a report here which says 'we had duck *à l'orange* made with Cooper's marmalade'. Quite often they'll just put tinned mandarin oranges on an ordinary piece of duck.

What about wine?
Part of my job is to find out how much a wine waiter knows. I find that if you make a friend of the wine waiter you can

find out more from him than anyone else around, because he has plenty of time to stand around and watch. Some of them have really been quite well-trained. There are these excellent courses run by the Wine and Spirit Association and hundreds of youngsters go there and get more than a basic training. But, of course, there are great gaps. One report said, 'the waitress was heard asking a friend what a "giraffe" of wine was'.

How difficult is it for a place to get into the Guide?
Well, let's put it like this. There are no good restaurants in Britain that we don't know about, and when a new one starts up we immediately hear about it through our members. After all these years, we have got to know who are the reliable members, and if a new place sounds promising, one that they have recommended, we put it on what we call a private list which goes only to our voluntary inspectors. We've got about 160 of those all over the country – I used to be one before I came on the staff. They get these lists two or three times a year, and it's their job voluntarily to go to any that are in their neighbourhood. That means that these potentially good places are really properly inspected.

What happens after that?
Well one sees how it goes during the year. We're getting constant reports from our members and then if there's any doubt about the place, if the reports are conflicting for instance during the last three months before the *Guide* comes out, we'll send a paid inspector who'll case the joint properly and fill in a very detailed form.
The inspectors are people very carefully selected from among those who have been reporting regularly to us for some years. They won't necessarily have had a career in catering or have done a course on wine, though some of them have, but they are people who have got a great interest in food and wine, and who eat out frequently. Most of them have sent in some

hundreds of reports before they are even considered. They may be employed for two or three months by us full time.

How do you set about making a report?
I always try to go alone to a place, and I avoid getting into conversation with people. If you turn it into a social occasion, you quickly find that people are asking what you do. I usually go into the bar first, if there is one, because you can find out a lot from a barman. Then into the restaurant – I don't mind being placed near the kitchen, you can pick up quite a bit by being there. I have a half bottle of wine with the meal, and then one just eats and observes and, because you are working, you take more in than the casual diner.

Do you find the Guide excites hostility among caterers?
There is now very little hostility at all. In fact, when the last *Guide* was being prepared, we had more letters than we could count from innkeepers thanking us for bringing them so much business, and we're often rung up by new places asking how they can get in the *Guide*. We tell them that it's a question of waiting, and if they are good, there will be favourable reports and in due time they may have an entry. But although they know they can't buy their way in, you'd be surprised how many people put their friends up to sending in reports. Strangely enough you can always recognize a report that has been sent in by a friend of the proprietor. Somehow the language used gives it away immediately.

You have over 1,600 entries. Do you think there should be more?
If we lowered our standards there could be, but I would say there are something like 7,000 restaurants which, if they raised their standards, could become eligible for entry. Let's face it, they don't get much incentive. A vast number of people just don't care what they eat. You'll get a restaurant owner breaking his heart trying to provide something unusual and nobody asks for it – they go in for their fish and

chips or steak and chips . . . it's always chips. A vast mass of our population, as far as I can make out, eat nothing but chips with absolutely everything. People don't seem to care much about taste either. A great number of people measure a meal by quantity, not quality. They'll say: 'I had a marvellous meal. My plate was absolutely covered!' I honestly think they often go for the look of a meal, not the taste.

Is it that people don't care or that they don't like to complain?
Maybe a bit of both. I made a scene once on British Rail. I was going up to a committee meeting in Manchester, and had lunch on the way. The coffee was even worse than usual, it tasted of iron filings. I complained about this, and they apologized and brought me another cup exactly the same, still tasting of iron filings. Everybody else was drinking it quite happily without any fuss. After the meeting, we got on the train and went into the dining-car and it was the same crew. One of them came up to me and said, 'Oh, sir, about the coffee. We found out why it tasted like it did. You see, we put the coffee pot on the corner of the stove and the extraction hood is rather rusty and the condensation was running along the edge of the hood and into the coffee pot.' But although it tasted really foul, nobody else seemed to have noticed it.

Have you any theories about why good restaurants often deteriorate so quickly?
Well, if they do fall off, it's probably because we don't have a family tradition in this country. In France most restaurants are family concerns, handed down from father to son. Here you could count the places like that on the fingers of one hand. So it often happens that when an individual sells, the restaurant is bought by someone who either doesn't care or doesn't know.

Don't you think by recommending places, you can very often destroy them?
We've been told of one place that had to close because it got

too much business, and blamed the *Guide* entry. More often, I think, you will get the hotel-keeper put on his mettle to keep his standards up. However, we have been told of places where an innkeeper says to himself, 'Good – now I'm in the *Guide* I can put my prices up and go slack on my service because my fortune's made', then in the next issue he's out, and he realizes that so far from being smart, he's not been clever at all.

Is the number of restaurants in the Guide likely to go up in the future, or will it remain around the 1,600 mark?
We think it will probably go up if our standards remain the same, but there is a good deal to be said for the theory that we ought to make our standards stiffer each issue.

If you're interested in food, it's certainly most unwise to venture out of doors without a copy of the current *Guide*. You may not always have the perfect meal, but at least you stand a better chance than if you just took pot-luck at the first place you came to. There are people who consider the *Guide* to be just a bit too precious; there are other people, like myself, who wish there weren't a law of libel so that the Consumers' Association could print some of the really appalling reports they receive from discontented members – a sort of Not so Good Food Guide . . .

THE WATCHED POT

Major and Mrs Rodney Immington-Jones have worked hard to merit their inclusion in this year's guide. The service is personal – Mrs Immington-Jones waits single-handed on the 40-odd tables, assisted during holiday time by Niobe and Hero, her school-age daughters. With its modest cost (all main courses under a guinea) The Watched Pot is a must for travellers to the West. There are over 375 items on the hand-printed menu, all of which can be served in three minutes, many of them being composite dishes tastefully presented in their original tin-foil containers. There is a wide selection of out of season vegetables served piping hot, with a knob of real butter. Try, particularly, the fish fingers and the remarkable selection of instant soups, garnished with chives.

BIDE-A-WEE

A bit off the main road from Spume to Bileleigh (turn left at the rustic sign), Miss Piggott and Miss Legge have turned this olde cottage into a delightful light luncheon and tea-room. Very popular with American visitors, the Bide-a-Wee boasts that everything it serves is fresh and home-made. All is good, solid English food here, from the substantial scones to the thick crusts of wholesome wholemeal bread.
The special 5s 9d lunch has received many commendations particularly from older members who don't want large helpings anyway. A sample lunch menu consisted of Bide-a-Wee soup (a tasty mixture of all sorts with a predominantly parsnip flavour), meat cutlet (made from an enterprising wartime recipe handed down to Miss Piggott by her nanny), croquette potatoes and kale, followed by a date and prune filled sponge pudding in a thick pastry crust, covered with whinberry sauce. 'A delightful experience,' writes one member who was most impressed with the gifted water colours executed in her spare time by the co-proprietrix, Ophelia Legge, whose father, Brigadier Lancing Legge, was a sometime exhibitor, between the two wars, at the Spume Water Colour Society. 'Don't miss walk in the garden after your meal,' writes M.H.J., 'but beware of the goat.'

CUILLIN VIEW

Almost equidistant between Muir of Ord, Boat of Garten, Crank of Strome and Kyle of Groat, this small guest house has been much recommended by visiting members. Mrs Maggie

Mackinnon keeps a good table and although guests are expected to attend punctually upon the gong (breakfast 8, lunch 12, high tea 6), meals are soon over, such is the speed of the service. In fact, one member who, caught in a Highland downpour, didn't return for lunch until twenty past twelve, found the dining-room deserted and her fellow guests already having their after meal cup of tea in the lounge. Mrs Mackinnon is a busy soul and likes to keep the place spotless. Guests are encouraged to go out and enjoy the delightful walking in the area which, especially on the few days when rain doesn't fall, can be exhilarating.

There is always Scotch broth for the mid-day meal and for the main course, either boiled mutton and 'neeps' or fried steak and onions. On Wednesday, when the Co-op van calls, Mrs Mackinnon usually gets in some frozen fish to vary the menu. This is followed by a choice of sweets: the changes are rung on fruit salad and Danish cream, blancmange, jelly and tinned pears, or, if Ma Mackinnon has had a heavy bake in recent days, one of her justly famous Strome trifles with a wee dram to give the custard a real Scots flavour. As one member wistfully observed, 'There's nae place like Strome'.

THE THREE ANGLERS

A fishy welcome awaits you at the Ing, Trilby, Dottel, Trueflower and Dreggs hostelry where genial mine host Commander 'Curly' Strangeways and his Good Lady, Bobby, preside over the new Smugglers Bar, aptly named in view of the area's long connection with the illicit trade in brandy and silks across the Channel. Old fishing gear and nautical trivia lend a delightful away-from-it-all note to this modern house. Curly's own collection of curios and relics from his naval days adorn the walls of the 'ship'. Even the toilets (Gulls and Buoys) have a nautical note. Commanders Special Keg, chilled under pressure, and served in pewter tankards, hot Grog and the Quarterdeck Cocktail (rum, orange and a little

of what you fancy) are the specialities. Try the fishcakes
(2s 9d), bangers in the basket (5s) and Cornish pasties (3s 6d).
Saturday night, Bobby puts on a special ten bob Wardroom
Buffet. Members have sent in enthusiastic reports. Mostly
open sandwiches (known in the Anglers as 'Bobby's Wedges')
the coverings are usually 'hot' and tasty – sardine, Tabasco,
chutney, cocktail shrimps, scampi, hardboiled egg, Cheddar
and pickles. There's usually a packed house at Sunday
lunchtimes and, to save time, the only drink served is pink
gin – with optional tomato juice for those in Hangover
Corner. Either Curly or Bobby, or usually both, are on tomato
juice, but they buck up and are back on the gin by closing
time.

LA DOLCE VITA

A newly opened Italian-style restaurant has won general
approbation from our more cosmopolitan members. Run by
two actors, the decor is 'op' and the lighting low. Everything
is served on Tuscan wooden platters, and what isn't on plates
and too runny appears in woven baskets. Ben does the cooking
and Leander waits at table. As Leander waits alone, the
periods between arriving and ordering, and ordering and
eating, and eating and leaving are, perhaps, as one member
uncharitably put it 'inordinate', but most members think the
partners are wise to keep it a 'family' business. In between
waiting and clearing the tables and washing up, Leander sells
Victoriana and bric-à-brac to foreign tourists and sings to a
small banjo.
The menu is unique in that Ben only does one dish per night.
This is likely to be a large earthenware pot of something with
lots of tomato, aubergine, garlic and olive oil – although
Leander tends to give it a different name each night. Thus,
members report having been offered *costa di manzo al vino
rosso, montone uso capriolo, capretto al vino bianco* and *carciofi alla
guidea* at various times. All these dishes seemed basically to be

vegetable stew, but quite pleasant. There is fruit to follow
and, when Ben can obtain it, cheese. Reports indicate that
there has been no coffee in recent months as the local grocer
has withdrawn his credit.

THE LITTLE BO-PEEP

This restaurant at Grimley is now under a change of
management. It has appeared in previous guides as 'The
Little Jack Horner' (1959), 'The Nell Gwynne' (1961), and
'The Cheshire Cat' (1964). The new owners have repainted
the premises lilac and orange throughout, and the food they
offer, although simple, well merits a place in these pages.
Despite their greater success with *rechauffé* dishes, the ice-creams
are reliable, as are the wide range of individual fruit pies
served hot in their cartons and piped invitingly with mock
cream. There is a special Snack lunch for those not requiring
a heavy mid-day repast, and here members have warmly
recommended a wide range of *sur toast* offerings: pilchards,
baked beans, spaghetti, *oeuf pochée*, welsh and buck rarebit,
tomatoes. These are all served with toast on the side, and
either a pot of tea or white coffee. The proprietors have
discontinued their attempt last year to do an evening meal.
As nobody goes out in the evening in Grimley, it was felt that
this sort of venture in *haute cuisine*, although profitable in
London and other large centres like nearby Ashtown, was not
economically viable for so small a place. In any case, most
people have had their evening meal by six-thirty and there
would not be much demand for a large three course supper,
the like of which THE LITTLE BO-PEEP had envisioned.

THE SATU EMPAT JALAN

When Beryl and 'Ginger' White left Malaya, they had little,
but Ginger's pension, (he had been rubber planting for 30
years,) and Beryl's indomitable cheeriness. Before she said

good-bye to her faithful old 'cookie,' she scribbled out a few of his recipes. Armed with these, the Whites opened this off-beat Malayan-style restaurant in the heart of Wessex. The specialities are very hot Malay, Indonesian and Indian curries. 'Too hot to eat,' as more than one member has reported. Mr White has built a Bamboo Bar where he serves in sarong and songkok (native religious hat). Lunches, or 'tiffins' as they are referred to, are not usually ready until about three, and on Sundays even later, but none of the regulars seem to mind. Most of them are happily occupied in the Bamboo Bar enjoying the gin 'pahits', long, cool and fairly lethal, of which Mr White is an adept and more than insistent dispenser. One or two members have reported that in the late evenings Mr White is inclined to be argumentative, particularly if, as one report put it, 'the sun has gone down early!'

'Unexpected' is the adjective one member applied to his visit, but those who appreciate good spirits and informality might do worse than give THE SATU EMPAT JALAN a try.

THE GALLEON

Situated right on the quay front in the quaint old world fishing village of Polzance, THE GALLEON finds its way into this year's guide with many endorsements. Although this gay and vivacious restaurant is housed in a traditional building, it is far from traditional inside. Passing through the front entrance hall, which is a combination of general stores and 'gifte shoppe', one enters the restaurant or cafeteria area proper. Here, smiling helpers hand out trays and one passes down an aisle packed with traditional dishes, starting with soup and ending at the far end of the counter by the tea and coffee urns. Members have singled out the Polzance pasties for special mention – one vegetarian member even claimed that their contents didn't infringe his own rigid dietary code. Pie and chips is perhaps the 'best buy', but the joint of the day, at 8s 6d, is a firm attraction for holiday makers. Also highly recommended, the macédoine of vegetables salad, creamed rice pudding, fig roll and homemade custard, and tea 'the colour of mahogany', as one member approvingly wrote. All guests are presented with a lucky Cornish pisky charm as they pay at the cash desks on the way out. At the rear of the cafeteria is a convenient play area for children with a wide choice of penny in the slot and fruit machines.

THE FLEET

This, one of the more exciting of London's new restaurants has only recently opened. The *mise-en-scène* designed by a young Italian is an almost too perfect replica of the old Fleet prison. The waiters are dressed as jailers, and the mugs and plates are all chained to the tables. In the centre of the restaurant, a replica of Tyburn gallows has been erected and here four chefs do a great quantity of *flambé* cooking. Illumination is provided by old lanterns. Customers are encouraged to come in period dress. Should this not be practicable, you can visit the 'tiring room' before going to your table. Here, for a small charge, you will be issued with wigs and ragged clothing before being skilfully made up by one of the Tiring Room Staff, an out-of-work actress. The Head Turnkey will then escort you to one of the cells opening off the main room, and present you with the Verdict. This varies from night to night. One member reports being 'sentenced' to a very pleasant 35s *table d'hôte* dinner of stewed eels, Ludgate tripe and *oranges à la Nell Gwynn*. There are glasses of malmsey and sack to drink as well as Small Beer and Ye Fleet Ale. There have been several complaints about the dampness of the restaurant. In his quest for authenticity, the designer has caused the fibre-glass stone walls to be occasionally flushed with water. Another member claimed to have slipped on the wet straw-covered floor and broken her ankle in three places. But every restaurant has its teething troubles. More reports from Debtors, please, on what sounds like a truly memorable evening's entertainment.

GREENSLEEVES

This mainly vegetarian restaurant has been enthusiastically recommended by members. Half-way between Oxford and Hampstead, it specializes in what the proprietors claim to be 'good honest food'. Mr Simon Allways (who must be the only Old Norse-speaking chef in that part of the world) is a former Cambridge don who, with his wife, Patty, decided to try and run a restaurant 'where you could jolly well be sure of good wholesome grub'.

Mrs Allways does amazing things with nuts, but most of the preparation of food, (there is little actual cooking), is done by her husband. Usually on the menu is dock and nettle salad (3s 6d) and a selection of raw vegetable juices squeezed on the spot. The cereal rissoles are fun as are the wholenut bran cakes and Vitafrute pudding all at 5s. As the Allways try to serve nothing but fresh food, which they have grown or picked themselves, the best time to visit them is in the summer when field and hedgerow afford a cornucopia of good things. One member, who arrived for lunch in mid-winter, was offered a turnip omelette which he found far from sustaining. However, specialized cooking of this kind is very demanding, and members are asked to ring Chard Forridge 41 well in advance to discuss their dietary requirements. To fit in with Mr Allways' teaching commitments, the restaurant is not open on Thurdsay, Tuesday evenings, the first and last Wednesday in the month, alternate Mondays, Fridays during term, Sundays from August to June and certain Saturdays.

The fourth largest industry

'What is missing, what really marks out the hotel and catering industry from many other modern British industries, can be summed up in a single word, and a word too often misunderstood in this country. That word is "professionalism." '

John Fuller, Director Scottish Hotel School, University of Strathclyde

They call it the fourth largest industry in Britain. 700,000 men and women work in catering. The turnover in 1964 was £2,350 million.

But nobody in Britain can tell you how many restaurants there are because no such survey has been undertaken. The British Travel Association thinks there are about 40,000 hotels and boarding houses in Britain. Board of Trade figures reveal that there are 68,905 public houses but it's not clear how many of these serve meals. We know that there are 32,523 restaurants, cafés and snack bars but where the snack bar graduates to a café and where the café becomes elevated to the status of a restaurant is again not known.

If this is the fourth largest industry in Britain, it must also be the one containing the most strange bed-fellows. It includes 17,234 fish and chip shops with a total turnover of £63 million; the Monjil Restaurant in Clarence Road, Southend-on-Sea, Essex, Directors Abdul Hussain Jaigirder and Lionel Tree, nominal capital £100; The Kentucky Pancake Kitchen chain operating 14 units with a turnover totalling £750,000; the Trust House group who serve a million meals a week in their 200 hotels and who, in 1965, had a pre-tax profit of £2·17 million; 30,000 industrial canteens serving 2,300 million meals a year; Golden Egg Restaurant (Holdings) Ltd. which achieved pre-tax profits of £216,000 for the last six months of 1965; the New Sea Chinese Restaurant, Lumley Road, Skegness, run by Wong Kam Lin, Wong Cheong Yau, Lee Wong Tai, Tsang Kam Chuen and Sau Lum Tsang; Grand Metropolitan Hotels, whose profits before tax in 1965 were £2 million; 3,900 catering contractors with an annual turnover of £30 million; Parkes Restaurant in Beauchamp Place, London where dinner for two costs between £7 and £10 – and Sam's place on the Great North Road where you can get a plate of hot nosh for 5s 6d. It includes such diverse characters as Sir Geoffrey Crowther, 65-year-old chairman of Trust Houses who describes his recreations as 'places, music and history' and

18-year-old Gary Anthony Wade who, on Easter Monday 1966, made £7 8s 4d selling hot dogs from a stand near the old fish-market in Hastings and whose recreations are 'watching telly, going out with birds and mucking about with the bike.'

It is an industry which, particularly on the hotels and restaurants side, feels that successive post-war governments have powerfully discriminated against. It regards itself as part of 'Britain's fastest growth industry' – the tourist trade – even though it is demonstrable that only 10% of its activities cater for foreign tourists. When in May 1966 the Labour government introduced its selective employment tax there were sharp cries of protest. Faced with the prospect of paying a weekly tax of twenty-five shillings on every male employee and a twelve and six for every female, industry leaders predicted inevitable price increases. The *Hotel and Catering Times* called it, 'a black Budget with punitive vicious proposals which will do us irreparable harm.'

Caterers were not slow to react. The extra costs could not be taken out of profits they must be passed on to the customer. Said *The Caterer and Hotel-keeper*: 'prices charged to the public will have to go up to meet these additional heavy costs. But why wait until the blow falls, the new tax operates from September, so let us begin now to raise our prices, wherever we can, in a phased operation spread over the next four months'. This particular editorial on May 12th, 1966 claimed: 'it strengthens the view that our present rulers are actively hostile to this industry, which is even worse than the previous Government, who were merely deaf to our pleas'.

From the correspondence in the National and trade Press one might have assumed that the whole industry was on the verge of bankruptcy. It would not be unfair to say, as a community the hotel and restaurant men see themselves as a really hard-pressed group and they run the farmers a very close second in the Disaster Stakes. Measures are always 'punitive', concessions 'derisory'; each new fiscal move is 'the straw to break the camel's back'. The industry's back is strangely resilient. Despite the prophecies of doom plenty of people can be found prepared to invest money in catering and there's no doubt some significant fortunes have been made despite the obstacles. Year by year the industry manages to struggle gamely on, putting a half-crown on here, another 3% on there. Are things really as bad as the spokesmen claim? There's at least one man in the industry who remains unperturbed. He is Mr R. McK. Bruestedt, proprietor of The Spread Eagle Hotel in Jedburgh who wrote to *The Caterer and Hotel-keeper* 12th June, 1966 with this plea:

'Let's have some cheery letters and look on the bright side of things. It's a great industry and none of us seem to starve and I suppose that before the Chancellor taxes us he will have had a very good look at our income tax returns and note that most of us can manage a good holiday or two a year. Tomorrow is a brand new day and even for all the moaners, I think life is still pretty good, if not better than ever. There are still a vast number of people going about with lots of money in their pockets. All you have to do is take it from them.'

Of course what's good for Jedburgh may not be good for the industry as a whole, but how homogeneous are the interests of the thousands of men and women who make up the industry? Their leaders tend to make generalizations as if they were talking about something which had a cohesive entity. The industry needs 'more work study on management techniques' I read the other day, but how does that apply to the little one-man fish and chip shops? 'Invest in training' advised another editorial, but would that improve all those cafés selling cups of tea and egg and chips? 'Planning is essential for survival' said another headline, but how would planning have helped the survival of the Blue Beat Coffee Bar, 144 Ocean Road, South Shields, Durham, on whose proprietor a Receiving Order and Order of Adjudication were made on February 1st, 1966?

The industry is thousands and thousands of Italians, Indians, Spaniards, Portuguese, Pakistanis, Cypriots, West Indians, Chinese, and Greeks waiting at table, scrubbing, cooking good and bad food, washing up and working under sometimes filthy conditions. It's lots of somebody's mum cooking toad in the hole and rice pudding in great echoing canteens. It's thousands of waitresses of all sizes and colours rushing about with pots of tea and scones in department stores. It's publicans' wives doing lunch-time snacks of shepherd's pie and baked beans. It's Wimpy Bars, Golden Eggs, hospital kitchens, the Dorchester, sandwich-bars, Express Dairies, meals-on-wheels, Fortes, Berni's, Chicken Inns, ice-cream parlours, Kardomahs, steak houses, fish bars, whelks on stalls, workmen's cafés, banquets and balls, weddings and factory outings, masonics, tea tents, bed and breakfast, the Savoy Grill, and the Savoy Café and Snack Bar Coaches Welcome, set lunches, cut off the joint and two veg, *table d'hôte, a la carte*, help yourself, vendomats, luncheon vouchers . . .

It's an industry which inspires great loyalty. Many at the top of this Tower of Babel feel there's nothing much wrong with it. When, in the early stages of writing this book, I rang up the British Hotels and Restaurants Association, the B.H.R.A., a peculiar thing happened. I talked to the 'Director & Secretary', Eric D. Croft, M.B.E., M.A., B.Sc. and when I mentioned that one of the things I was interested in discussing with him was the reason why British food, internationally, had such a bad reputation, the atmosphere noticeably chilled. In fact, he wrote to me a few days later suggesting that a remark of that kind didn't do me much credit. He went further and told me that he didn't think it inspired confidence. He then revealed that there were already in existence many books about eating in Britain – written by *experts* – and he ended up by regretting that he couldn't ask any of his colleagues to spend their time assisting me. I began to wonder why a suggestion that perhaps all was not well with the industry was not thought worth discussing. Was there something to be concealed? Far from daunting me in my labours, this official brush-off gave me renewed vigour and I burrowed even deeper into the files.

I found that Eric D. Croft wasn't the only person who thought that eating out in Britain was satisfactory. In 1965, for instance, Lord Geddes made a public pronouncement about our food which no doubt pleased the Director & Secretary of the B.H.R.A. deeply. As Chairman of the British Travel Association he stated: 'Our restaurants these days are providing standards of cooking and service as good as any to be found on the continent'. In the same year Sir Ian Fraser, M.P., at the summer meeting of the Association of Health and Pleasure Resorts in Morecambe, declared: 'No food in the world is as good as English food!' A sweeping statement? Sir Ian must have thought so because he added an afterthought, '– if it's properly cooked and served on hot plates'.

1965 was a vintage year for compliments. In May, Mr Desmond Hopkinson, Chairman of the Association of British Travel Agents, told a meeting of the Hotel Sales Managers Association:

'Generalizing, I am sure that it is right to say that the standard of restaurant food has risen by leaps and bounds in this country until it is now *comparable with that of any other country.*'

(My italics.) Laying it on too thick, perhaps? I don't suppose Mr Hopkinson really meant that our restaurants in the Thames Valley are comparable with those in the Loire, or that the restaurants of Devon are comparable with those of the Dordogne or Liverpool with Lyons or Buckinghamshire with Burgundy. In fact, when I went to see him the other day, he drew my attention to something else he's said on the same occasion:

'True, some of the leaps and bounds have been over establishments who still have the effrontery to cut a cold

joint with a razor, pour hot gravy over it and serve it as
roast beef, to be followed by "trifle" – stale cake, a dollop of
jam and a covering of cracked custard.'

The trouble is that if some unsuspecting foreigner did wander
into one of the many thousands of places specializing in that
sort of effrontery he might wonder what Mr Hopkinson meant
by saying our food 'is now comparable with that of any other
country'. You can't, I would have thought, have it both ways.
You can't criticize the industry in one sentence and tell us
that its standards are comparable with any other country in
the next. But criticism, in some quarters, is not welcome.
Mr Edward Heath, opening the 1966 Hotelympia, said:
'Criticisms of British hotels and food are to a great extent
misplaced'. A reassuring and politic remark to make,
surrounded as he was by the top brass of 'the fourth largest
industry'. But where are the criticisms to be placed? Perhaps
at the feet of the image-makers who have conjured up a
picture of British food which exists only in the mind.
An interesting side-light on the creation of this illusion was
revealed by Mr Conrad Jameson in a talk he gave to the
Hotel Sales Managers Association in February 1965. His
theme: 'Motivation in the Service of the Hotel Industry'.
During it, he described in some detail the advertising
campaign planned by David Ogilvy to persuade Americans to
come to Britain:

'The favourite criticism of Americans was British food. One
is tempted to say that they tended to imagine British food was
almost as bad as it usually is . . . But perhaps it would be
kinder to point out that Americans have a roast beef of old
England story-book version of this country in their minds.
England for Americans is the England of Dickens they read
about in school . . . Ogilvy didn't try to fight these American
fantasies about Britain . . . he probed them in depth. He asked
people to describe the kind of hearty English fare you could
expect in the old days – and then proceeded to *play back*

these fantasies to Americans in a brilliant series of *New Yorker* advertisements. The fantasy image used by Ogilvy looks like a kind of Hollywood version of an English pub: salmon and pheasant and quail and foaming tankards of beer and thirty kinds of indigenous cheese and that sort of thing . . . Ogilvy did nothing to change British food; he performed essentially a grease-paint operation to make it appear better than it is. Might I point out that trying to grease-paint a product into success is more likely to work when your customers are 3,000 miles away and can't examine the product for themselves.'

In fairness I should record that the British Travel Association do not accept the suggestion that they deliberately publicized false images of Britain. They told me: 'After 20 years of operating the "Come to Britain" campaign, we are now receiving more and more "repeat" visitors – people who have been here once, liked what they were offered, and have travelled thousands of miles to come again!' Whether they return to Britain despite the grim prospect of facing British food is not known. The B.T.A. do have complaints about British food, but strangely they claimed, 'most of the people who do the complaining are, in fact, British themselves – most of whom are quite content to eat some of the abominable muck served up in other countries just because it is foreign and has a foreign name and, therefore, must be good'.
It's an industry that excites women like Lady Lewisham, to get up in public and say: 'We in Britain have the best food and the worst cooks . . . the crimes which are committed in this country against food should be a hanging offence'. It's an industry which suffers from the honesty of *The Good Food Guide* which, after an 18 year search extended to Ireland and the Channel Isles, can only find 1,600 places worth eating in. And, if you're interested in statistics, that means for every 35,000 people in the area there's only one establishment where they stand a chance of getting a good meal. As

Raymond Postgate says of what he calls 'the continuing inadequacies of British catering':

'The first, and largest of all, is that it is still on the whole bad. Bad on the average . . . you cannot reckon that if you call in at any good-looking place you will have a decently cooked meal even if there is no great choice. What you will have is a meal whose ingredients have been spoiled by wretched cooking; and it will be indolently served, or worse.'

It's an industry which recently found itself short of nearly 50,000 trained staff. A manpower research project, undertaken by B.H.R.A. among its members, found that waiters were 22·5% below establishment, porters 24·5% and kitchen staff 24·9%. It is the only industry where the amateur is able to command more respect than the professional. Some of the best small restaurants in Britain today are run by men and women who just happen to like food. It is accepted that an ex-Squadron Leader and his wife will probably give you a better meal than a professional chef. Brigadiers blithely take on ten-roomed hotels and colonels are discovered bent over the *bain-marie*. Many people in the industry acknowledge that the 'amateur' is often far more dedicated and renders a greater service to the community than the professional caterer. One such amateur is a man who bought an empty house and turned it into a hotel in 1963, 'and to judge by both bookings and the plaudits of guests from all over the world I appear to be making a success of it without any professional experience whatsoever'. In a letter to a trade journal he described a meal taken in a Brighton hotel run by 'professionals':

'In a beautiful and uncrowded dining-room (of which I was thoroughly envious) we were served an absolutely disgusting lunch, of which the only good item of three courses for seven people was fresh melon. The service by *very* amateur continental students was a complete shambles, and we were charged 15s 6d for a three course lunch, (the final course a soggy bottled-fruit pudding sloshed on a plate swimming in custard made without milk,) which I would have been ashamed to offer in my amateur establishment, where we charge 10s 6d for a three course, well-cooked and attractively presented and served meal including fresh cream instead of the ghastly custard which is so notorious a part of British cooking. Need I add any comment?'

When it comes to writing about food, it's a positive *dis*advantage to have had any professional training, or if you have had any, it pays to conceal it. When Robert Carrier, resident food writer of the *Sunday Times* took a few weeks off, the editors got a man called John Addey to take his place. 'He is a Yorkshireman living in London. He is a barrister by training, stood for Parliament in the last two elections and runs a business consultancy.' There was no mention anywhere that he had received formal training in cooking which presumably gave him a flying start over a professional chef.

It's an industry which is living in two centuries. At one end there are still the great hotel kitchens with their *brigades de cuisine*, each member with his own specialized job to do, conscious of an immutable pecking order. Here traditions are strong and jealously guarded. At the other end there are the growing number of eating places where what cooking there is, (heating a hamburger or frying an egg,) can be done by unskilled labour. There are places where they still prepare food the way they did for Edward VII: there are places where all that's needed is enough strength to open a refrigerator door.

Even though there are 164 catering schools and colleges in the country where over 10,000 students are attending full-time courses there is a remarkably high rate of wastage. A man very concerned with education in the industry told me:

'You have people coming out of the technical colleges into

the industry and they get disillusioned. The conditions of work are poor – in fact, if you look at some of the working conditions, the way the staff are treated almost suggests that those in authority consider that the workers are servile. You won't get anywhere in this industry until people in management are convinced of the importance of giving their staff good working conditions. There's a large number of people who would get a great deal of satisfaction out of serving people and producing good food, but they find the conditions are poor. Another industry, for which they *haven't* been trained, offers them better wages and conditions and off they go. I don't blame people for getting out.'

In the spring of 1966, a conference was organized in London by G.S.M.S., (the Graduate and Student Management Society). At this conference many critical voices were raised against the lack of planning and dynamism in the industry. L. H. Bond, Chief Personnel Officer of Trust Houses, lashed out at employers. 'British employers are lazy and self-indulgent. They have become insular and introvert, and do not realize the seriousness of the current staff crises in this country . . . it is astounding that our industry has for so long neglected what is obviously the most important aspect of our business.' Bond pointed out that in the past, the industry had relied on continental workers, particularly men and women attracted from countries with a lower standard of living. But that labour supply was drying up. Bond prophesied that all conditions of employment would have to be looked at very soon. At the moment, he claimed: 'the value and capital investment in human beings has less priority than a piece of furniture'. Another paper claimed that labour in the industry wasn't employed to its maximum efficiency: 'If we regard the effective training of employees as a measure of efficiency, the industry is a highly inefficient employer. Little or no proper training is carried out.' The paper went on to ask:

'Who is to do the essential research into the industry, so that

168

there is a constant and reliable flow of information? Who is going to accurately forecast manpower requirements? Who is to exert positive pressure to improve industrial relations?'

The conclusion of this particular report, written by Peter Venison, Assistant Manager of the Carlton Tower, London, Roger Doswell, Kobler Research Fellow at the Battersea College of Technology and Miles Quest, Features Editor of *The Hotel and Catering Times*, ran thus:

'What is needed is a positive commitment that staff and management must be trained and developed . . . Until this has been accepted, the industry's future remains, quite literally in jeopardy.'

An alphabet of eating out

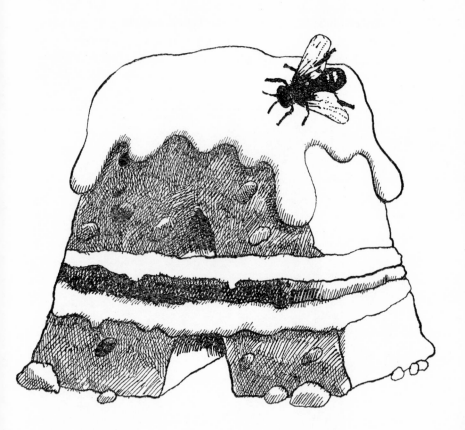

Apples, or any kind of fresh fruit, are not come by easily in our restaurants. This surprises many foreign visitors, especially those who come by boat-train in the summer through the Garden of England and see the Kentish fruit-trees burdened with apples and pears and plums. They expect to find great bowls of fruit brought to the table – instead of which they're offered tinned fruit salad or tinned pears or tinned lychees or anything except our own native produce. It is not economic to buy fresh fruit I'm told, 'People don't want it'. An exception to the no-fresh-fruit rule is strawberries. When there's a good year even the cheapest café will offer strawberries and 'cream'. See CREAM.

Beef is expensive. It is more expensive than chicken. And yet this change in the relative prices of chicken and beef is not always reflected in prices. In the Spring of 1966 a Colchester restaurant was still charging 6s 6d for chicken and salad and only 5s 6d for roast beef and salad. When I asked the manager why, he agreed that the prices should have been the other way round but explained that the traditional approach to chicken still persisted, chicken was still regarded as a luxury meat – a useful illustration of how both consumer and caterer are fettered by the past.

Breakfast is best eaten in small country inns where one woman is cooking for a small number of people. The toast will be fresh and you'll get a splendid plate of bacon, eggs, mushroom, sausage and tomato sizzling hot from the stove. The average hotel breakfast is not like that. If you ask for fried egg it will probably have been cooked some time before and kept warm in an oven – it will have a blanched appearance, like one of those celluloid eggs you get in Joke Shops. Most hotel breakfasts taste as if they have been cooked in the small hours of the morning and left lying about. Refuse tinned grapefruit segments and bottled fruit juices. Avoid porridge except in Scotland. The tea is likely to be fresher than the coffee. Of ten large hotels in which I have taken breakfast in the last twelve months only one, the Caledonian Hotel in Aberdeen, provided me with a well-cooked breakfast. As I had to catch an early plane to London my breakfast was cooked to order at six in the morning by the hall porter who knew what he was about.

Butter 'Is butter still rationed in England?', a visitor asked me after her first meal in London. Butter is no longer rationed – it just seems to be. Favourite way of serving it is in a deceptive-looking earthenware pot. The pot looks big and deep but when you put your knife into it you find it's extremely shallow and contains an inadequate amount of butter. Most people do not like to ask for more – the pot is therefore very popular among caterers as a form of portion-control.

Chicken used to be a childhood treat. Today it's all too often some deep-frozen, hormone-fed factory bird, very tender and almost entirely tasteless. Now and again when things go wrong in the factory the dead chicken has a faint flavour of haddock. Chicken aficionados should look out for a new taste sensation just imported from America. It's 'Instant Chicken', available in $2\frac{1}{2}$ lb. white meat and 6 lb. white and dark meat rolls. 'Absolutely no wastage,' runs the trade press advertisement, 'it's all chicken. No cooking needed – it's already cooked. No bones – makes carving obsolete, slices perfectly – ensures 100% accurate portion control'.

Chicory is the curse of the coffee-drinking classes in Britain. Chicory (Cichorium intybus) has a long fleshy taproot which when roasted and ground can be used as an adulterant for coffee. It gives coffee additional colouring and that extremely unpleasant bitter taste prized by British palates.

Chips Lyons, a group who are renowned for their highly accurate research into what the eating public wants have recently opened a restaurant in Chancery Lane, London, called 'Chips With Everything'. For a shilling you can get as many chips as you like with your Hamburger (10d), Bacon, (10d), egg (10d) tomatoes (6d), beans (6d). You could even have chips with your fruit pie, gâteau or dessert surprise and I doubt if the management would mind if you did. 'Chips' was designed to appeal to the younger set whose favourite haunts are the Kentuckys, the Golden Eggs and the Wimpy Houses. Lyons research revealed that teenagers 'wanted chips with practically everything'. The logical extension to the 'chips' house should surely be to add custard and gravy to the list of ubiquitous offerings. If you eat in a works canteen, as millions of men and women do every day, you will be offered not only chips with every main course dish but a generous ladle of 'gravy'. It's a sort of all-purpose brown-mix which does nicely over beef, lamb, veal, chop, pie, mince – anything. There is also an all-purpose custard which can be put on any and every pudding. But as Lyons have found: chips, gravy, custard, these three; the greatest of these is still chips.

Coffee The British like their coffee to be the colour of fudge and take it reinforced with spoonfuls of white sugar. The proper way to make English coffee is to buy a tin of coffee powder, or a bottle of coffee extract, and add a teaspoonful to a cup of boiling milk or milk diluted with water. 'Coffee' is now easier to make than tea and it's popularity has grown to such an extent that in a recent survey 59% of the people questioned claimed they would drink coffee when eating out, only 18% tea. Coffee has always been a socially superior drink to tea. As Billy Liar said of the Southerners, 'They don't drink tea down there, it's all coffee!' Although nobody, except perhaps a caterer, would dream of re-boiling tea, it is common practice to re-heat coffee. One Tuesday last year a guest in a Midland hotel complained that the coffee tasted horrible. 'It shouldn't', said the waitress, 'it was only made on Friday!' If in doubt, drink tea.

Cost control is the system whereby the caterer ensures that he is charging the right amount for what he is giving. Seeing that everyone gets exactly what they pay for is also known as portion control. Portion control in action is that little foil-wrapped pack of butter on your table, containing precisely ten grammes of butter. Carried to its ultimate it can turn the operation of a hotel into one calling for almost military precision and detailed advance planning. An article in a trade journal described recently how a hotelier had virtually done away with swill bins by using cost control. To him swill bins were a sign of waste, and waste was money down the drain. His routine was childishly simple. He had a fortnightly menu plan, a specially compiled recipe book and his Arrival and Departure (A & D) lists. The recipe book breaks the fortnightly cycle of menus (most guests don't stay longer) into fixed portions of each ingredient per serving. By consulting the A & D list you order and prepare exactly the right quantity of food needed for each guest – each day's catering is planned two weeks in advance. If an item becomes too costly a more economic alternative is used. Frozen vegetables are ordered in bulk and then weighed out in set portions. Instant coffee is used to permit strict quantity control and is served in cups giving seven to the pint. To ensure that each guest receives precisely $1\frac{1}{2}$ ounces of potato salad they use an ice-cream scoop and if all the mathematics have been properly done, when the last guest has received the last ration, the saucepan should be empty. When serving roast beef each guest is given a two-ounce portion, neither more nor less. Left-overs are used to make savoury cutlets or vegetable soup. It sounds ideal from the cost-control angle. But what happens if a guest asks for more?

Custard Britain's second favourite food. Custard can be ladled on any pudding you care to name. It ranges in colour from almost white to a violent plastic yellow reminiscent of war-time gas warning signs. Many people like it with lumps in, a culinary effect achieved by not bothering to mix it properly. Custard used to be made with milk, eggs and sugar. It is now made universally with custard powder which can be bought in hundredweight paper sacks. Custard fills the two great requirements of our Island Palate – it is sweet and filling.

Cream As all of us know, cream is the oily or butyraceous part of milk. It also comes in other forms. It can arrive in a tin tasting faintly metallic, or it can in some cases be evaporated milk – this is known as 'cream' because it has a creamy colour. There is also 'dairy cream', named no doubt to distinguish it from cream made with pig's fat or fishheads or some other money-saving left-over. There is also a fairly new product on the market which many people prefer to real cream. It doesn't pretend to be cream but it can be used as a cream substitute. It's called Dream Topping. It comes in the form of a powder, (the product is manufactured in America and packeted in England,) and the legend on the side of the packet claims, 'it can be served lavishly with fresh, canned or stewed fruit and is delicious with jellies and trifles'. There is a mouth-watering photograph on the packet of a great creamy dollop of Dream Topping crowning a pile of succulent strawberries. Dream Topping is made of hydrogenated vegetable oil, sugar, sodium caseinate, propylene glycol monopalmitate, hydroxylated lecithin, flavour and colour. But for a cream product which makes the incident of the loaves and fishes almost picayune by comparison we must turn to the British Oxygen Company which offers a miraculous invention called the Spark Whip Cream Whipper. 'If you've ever wondered how to serve whipped cream often, easily and with a very much higher return, wonder no longer!' The secret is the Spark Whip Bulb (50 for 29s) which aerates quite a little into quite a lot. All you do is put half a pint of cream and half a pint of milk into a special container, screw in a bulb 'and there you are! 4 pints of fresh whipped cream – yours to serve at the touch of a trigger'. I must say the publicity is very enticing – from the caterer's point of view: 'Whip up your profits with a Spark Whip cream whipper . . . it's today's way to whipped cream profits . . . the handiest Cream Whipper in the Catering Trade – with probably the biggest payoff'. The effect of the Whipper is to give you the impression that you are getting eight times more cream than you are, which accounts for its wide use in the industry.

Dogs are welcome in most eating places. Waitresses will often bend down to stroke them before handling your food. Some faddy people object – they don't think pets should be allowed in kitchens either. But have you thought how useful cats are for catching mice and cockroaches in dirty kitchens? So spare a kind thought for old puss fighting in the frontline of the war against dirt. His vigilance keeps Britain's kitchens fairly clean!

Fish is usually served in batter (fish and chip shop style) or in bright pink crumbs which lend a gritty taste to the meal. To get fish without either batter or crumbs is more difficult than you might think. In the ordinary café it is almost impossible. But when it comes to serving fish you learn not to be surprised at anything. I remember reading many years ago a book by Guy Gibson, V.C., about his war-time experiences in the R.A.F. He recalled how he and his wife, when staying at a country pub, received through the post a gift of smoked salmon from Scotland. They had to go to London but when they returned that evening they asked the landlord's wife if they could have their smoked salmon for supper. 'I'll just see if it's ready,' she said. A few minutes later she brought through two plates of hot smoked salmon fried in batter. The days are rapidly disappearing when you could be sure of being served fresh fish in seaside towns – but it's not a loss that many will notice, conditioned as they are to deep-frozen fish fingers and the eternal rubber-tasting scampi.

French is frequently crucified in the service of the English cuisine. I detect a theory in the catering trade that if you translate what you're selling into kitchen-French you can charge more for it and the customer will be more willing to excuse any shortcomings in the cooking – 'Perhaps that's how they have it in France'. I can't think of any other reason to account for such lunacies as, *Le Caneton D'Aylesbury, Le Grousse Rôtie, potage* of the day, *gâteau* cake, fruit and *crème, fromage* Stilton, *Le Poussin* Surrey, and sardine *sur* toast. Some French words are useful because they have no simple English equivalent – *bordelaise, chasseur, à la mode, provençale* – but the wholesale translation of a standard English menu into schoolboy French is both idiotic and annoying. On occasion French is used in such a grotesquely wrong way that it can only be construed as wilful ignorance or deliberate fraud. A few months back the Peterborough column in the *Daily Telegraph* printed a story which any student of the contemporary catering scene won't find surprising. A diner in a West Country hotel asked a waitress to give the chef his compliments and ask him why the pâté, described on the menu as a speciality of the house, appeared to have come out of a round tin. Three minutes later the waitress returned. 'I've had a word with Ernie,' she said 'and he says he's never seen *pâté maison* come in tins any other shape'.

Grousing is the only way to improve standards. It's no good writing a letter of complaint unless you have already complained on the spot. Complaining does not necessarily mean being offensive, although unfortunately complaining often appears to give offence and sometimes provokes a counter-attack from the employee. It is unreasonable to complain if someone is doing their best. If you are being charged an uneconomically low price for a meal and the meal is as a result bad, complaint is hardly justified. But if you feel you have been over-charged for inadequate food and service, reveal your grouse on the spot. If you feel justified, withhold payment – but be sure of your legal position first.

High Tea – inspired product of the British genius for compromise. A cross between tea and dinner/supper, it serves the welcome function of getting two meals over at once. Prime time for High Tea is 6 p.m. Seen at its best in Scotland and Ireland, countries which have never really given way to the fanciness of eating a big meal at eight o'clock at night. Traditional High Tea in Ireland is bread and butter, cakes and either ham and eggs or cold meat and salad. Many hotels in Scotland which serve dinner in the summer for the benefit of tourists revert to High Tea in October when the only visitors are commercial travellers. Pots of strong tea are drunk with this meal.

Joints A golden rule when eating out – if there's a joint on the menu have a cut off it and hope that it hasn't all been pre-sliced in a bacon machine and re-heated. Our English meat from New Zealand and Argentina is justifiably renowned throughout Europe.

Ice-Cream Modern ice-cream is the caterer's best friend. A recent trade advertisement read, 'Wall's introduce another sweet profit winner . . . these new shapes have the soft golden taste your customers most prefer. They cost 4s 4d each . . . and with a few extras can be turned into really profitable lines. Wall's new Dairy Shapes are pre-portioned and each is sling wrapped for easy serving. No wonder some caterers serve only ice-cream for sweet. It pays them.' So next time you go out for a meal and find there's only ice-cream for sweet you'll know at least one of the reasons why!

Left-Overs 'Made up main dishes are better than individual cuts of meat,' said an article in *The Hotel and Catering Times* recently. It added, 'there is far more profit on a portion of shepherd's pie than on a pork chop'. In front of me I have a pamphlet issued by the Flour Advisory Council. It contains 'eight imaginative answers to that constant cry "What shall I make with the left-overs?"' Many people might say you shouldn't make anything with the left-overs, but there's profit in puddings and pies and patties made from unused meat and veg.

Legally if you're poisoned by bad food in a restaurant you don't stand much chance of redress. Not if one is to go by the experience of a London woman who claimed that she had spent three weeks in bed and lost a stone in weight after eating bad snails. She brought an action for damages against the restaurant which had laid her low. Although she had the deep sympathy of the court, that was about all she did have. The case was thrown out and she had to pay the costs of the preliminary hearings. As the judge said, 'The plaintiff suffered what was quite clearly – if the statement of facts is correct – a very nasty illness and was ill for five months.' The judge remarked that the casual observer might think it odd the plaintiff was without remedy. 'This is due to the popular delusion that is floating about that when somebody suffers a calamity of some sort somebody else had got to pay for it . . . in point of fact the general rule is that the tree lies where it falls.' I must say, had she been living in seventh-century China this woman would have got slightly more satisfaction. In the days of the T'ang dynasty the law said: 'When dried or fresh meats cause a man to become ill all left-over portions should be speedily buried. The violator will be flogged with 90 strokes. He who deliberately gives or sells it to another will be banished for a year, and if the person to whom it is given or sold dies, the offender will be hanged.'

Oriental Restaurants, Indian, Pakistani and Chinese, are still on the increase. The majority of them serve a Europeanized version of Eastern food. Most popular are

Chinese restaurants. For every one person who eats in an Indian restaurant, four eat what they fondly assume to be Chinese food. The Chinese, a talented and industrious people, have observed that the British like their food well-cooked. As the essence of Chinese cooking is to steam or boil or fry it for the shortest possible time there is a basic conflict. What results is dish after dish of bean sprouts in a soya sauce gravy sprinkled with chicken and almonds, sliced beef, boiled pork, or boiled prawns, depending on what you've ordered. 67, 148, and 93 have one thing in common, they taste as if they've been stewing all day. Perhaps the most fascinating aspect of provincial Chinese restaurants are their attempts at preparing English food. Lamb chop, chips and peas is the usual speciality, the chop baked until hard, the chips large and greasy, the peas bright green. That considerable numbers of rational people should go out of their way to consume this kind of 'English' food in a Chinese restaurant is a tribute to the resilience of the British palate and must occasion a few inscrutably raised eyebrows in the kitchens where it's concocted.

Porridge It was E. M. Forster who wrote, 'Porridge fills the Englishman up, prunes clear him out, so their functions are opposed. But their spirit is the same: they eschew pleasure and consider delicacy immoral.' In Scotland porridge can still be obtained properly prepared, in England seldom. The English cook it without salt and treat it like a pudding, sprinkling sugar all over it. In a Highland hotel I once saw an American pour Corn Flakes over his porridge. The comment of the waitress was charitable; 'Well he's on holiday and he's enjoying himself poor soul.'

Quickness is the thing most Britons look for in their infrequent ordeals of eating out. As in a doctor's waiting-room, a jealous eye is kept on who came first and a meal can become an occasion of torment if somebody who sat down after you gets their tinned ox-tail soup first. If you want to be very British you say politely but firmly to the waitress, 'I think we were before those people!' That immediately establishes the fact that you are not the sort of person who can be pushed around. It won't make the food any better of course, but at least you can get out in double quick time.

Railways People are always complaining about the food they get on trains. They don't seem to see the fatuity of expecting to get perfectly cooked meals issuing from a tiny kitchen racketing along at speeds up to one hundred miles an hour. The rule about eating on trains is 'you get what comes' – the fact that what comes is often not very good is beside the point. Dining-car crews tend to be autocratic and very much in command of the situation. A diner who recently said to his attendant, 'I'd like my steak well done please,' was told, '*All our steaks are well done, sir!*' Dining-car attendants are a loyal and close-knit team. Watching them at work is a constant source of pleasure; it's juggling, acrobatics, showmanship and panache rolled into a virtuoso high-speed comedy act. There are Chaplinesque over-tones which should not have escaped the constant traveller. Many of the serving gestures are slightly exaggerated, slightly larger than life, so that by the end of the meal you've begun to feel you have taken part in a Happening. Trays are held higher than is strictly necessary, the footwork is almost balletic; there's a great deal of swooping and bending and intricate elbowing. This delicacy and pseudo-gentility is offset by the shouting that goes on, a legacy from the days when trains were noisier than they are now. If the atmosphere generated is more of the mess-deck than the wardroom this is probably because a high proportion of the attendants have had connections with the sea. There is too the slight suggestion of Micawber – messjackets are sometimes not quite spotless, there is a fraying of cuffs. As in air travel, meals are frequently served at unconventional times – lunch at 11.30 a.m. for instance or dinner at 6 p.m. I don't know which crew holds the Plastic Beaker for serving a four course meal in the shortest possible time – there obviously is a trophy, otherwise there wouldn't be such keen competition to bring each meal to the earliest possible conclusion. The ultimate railway meal would be everything brought at once with bill and a handful of change at the ready.

Rice Pudding – a highly-prized British dish; it's pap-food really, often served with custard. Rice pudding is top of the Canteen bill and can be bought in tins. To illustrate the esteem in which this dish is held there's the splendid story of Mrs G. Churchill, a Stirchley housewife, who distinguished herself notably on a recent occasion when she had embarked on a day trip to the sea. As she sat in the train she suddenly remembered that she had left a rice pudding in the oven. With lightning decision she scribbled a note and threw it out of the window as the train flashed through Bromsgrove. It was picked up by an alert lengthman who rushed it to the nearest signal box. There a quick-witted signalman phoned control with the news. Control without delay got in touch with the Birmingham C.I.D. and the C.I.D. contacted Mrs Churchill's daughter Vera. Vera flew to her mother's home and saved the beloved pudding with only seconds to spare. A story which gives the lie to those who claim that we don't care deeply about food.

Sandwiches were invented by an Englishman, John Montagu Sandwich. His other claim to fame is that during the period when he ran the British Navy its corruption and incapacity were outstanding. Sandwiches can be a good stop-gap if the bread is eatable. Most sandwiches are made from pre-sliced factory bread, a sort of chewy wadding much favoured by the British housewife. Sandwiches are the staple food in pubs, although it's not always easy to get them. The following dialogue occurred in a pub which advertised itself as selling 'The Best Sandwiches in Town':

Me: *Have you any sandwiches?*
Barmaid: Well they're mostly all gone.
         What have you got left?
         Beef, ham, pork, egg . . .
         I'll have pork
         Sorry the pork's all gone!
         I'll have beef then
         You'll have to wait
         I don't mind waiting

Ten minutes went by and I asked the barmaid how they were doing.

         What's that love?
         I was wondering if my sandwiches were ready?
         What sandwiches were they love?
         Beef
         How many rounds did you want?
         Two rounds
         Wait a minute and I'll order them.

After she had served several more customers with drinks she shouted my order up the hatch. Some time elapsed and there was a shout from above. After a bit I told the barmaid that I thought my sandwiches might be ready if she pulled the dumb-waiter down. They were. When I bit into the first one there was a strong flavour of mustard.

         *I'm sorry but these sandwiches have got mustard in them
         and I don't like mustard*
         Well you should have said – she always puts mustard
         in them! I suppose I'll have to change them, she
         won't like that at all.

She shouted up the hatch about my not liking mustard and the whole episode was closed neatly by the voice from above which said, 'That was the last of the beef and it's past my time. Tell him to have a pie if he's so fussy!'

Sauces are greatly admired by the British. We like tomato sauce, Worcester sauce and salad cream. We like bottled mint sauce which often tastes like vinegarized straw and is coloured a brilliant green like a traffic light. On our frozen scampi we like bottled *sauce tartare*. We are also as previously noted partial to pouring gravy over everything especially when it has the consistency of heavy-duty engine oil. We like our sauces to come to the table in the bottle so that in between examining the other guests we can read the labels and memorize the lists of ingredients.

Soup Even in the best hotels it is rare to find soup made in the traditional way. What is commonly served as soup is a convenience product – thick, over ambitiously coloured, bland. Even the addition of chopped parsley or a spoonful of fresh cream cannot conceal its origin – a paper bag. The favourite British soup is tomato. Anyone who has made tomato soup knows that it's true colour is a rather dull grey-red. Manufacturers have been forced to colour their tomato soup orange to make it attractive and 'authentic'. In the same way tinned tomato juice has to be dyed the colour of what the Average Consumer thinks tomato juice ought to look like. Are we perhaps colour-blind as well as palate-blind?

Tea – the one thing we do really well and, so we're told, one of the most attractive propositions in catering. As the Tea Information Service claims in a recent booklet, 'Selling tea can be like printing your own money'. In a half-page advertisement in a trade journal they laid bare the cost and profit figures for 'a small restaurant using the recommended recipe of $1\frac{1}{2}$ ounces of tea to the gallon'. They claimed a gross profit of 82 % for cup service and 79·4 % for pot service. Not bad.

Unfood Large quantities of food produced today are so bland that they could be a substitute for anything. If custard weren't so sweet you might mistake it for soup and if the soup weren't so thick you might mistake it for some form of home decorating adhesive . . . Not only is it now impossible to tell margarine from butter, it's rapidly reaching the stage where it's impossible with the eyes shut to experience any taste at all.

Untaste Modern technology has created many foods which come near to being totally tasteless but none more so than the kind of synthetic cream found in cheap cakes. It has an eerie silvery glow and is the ultimate in Untaste. One can detect a presence in the mouth but it might as well be ectoplasm for all the sensation the taste buds receive. Large areas of catering have accepted Untaste as a successful criterion for popularity. Very soon now there'll be a TV commercial with this challenge: 'It's so marvellous not even *you* could taste it!'

Verbiage The craze for qualifying every item on some of the more pretentious menus is now too well established to need comment. I passed a Steakhouse the other day advertising 'Steakmaster Steaks'. How that translates into English I don't know. This sort of verbiage is more often than not consciously or unconsciously dishonest. Honesty would be refreshing. For instance how about an egg sandwich described in the New Verbiage, 'Half an artificially ripened, un-peeled imported tomato and a third of a ten-day old battery egg laid between two pieces of machine-sliced factory bread fastidiously scraped with oleo-margarine containing artificial flavouring'. Or how about 'powder-fresh milk, chemically dyed haddock, turnip jam, lard-rich ice-cream'. It would be pleasant to get back to the days when one could assume that if one were offered cream it was fresh and came from a dairy or that the Salmon was Scotch and came from Scotland. I'm waiting for the first restaurant to extend its rich, ripe prose from the food to the whole apparatus of the meal: 'this superb example of our chef's skill sliced with sturdy Stainless Sheffield steel, gentled onto handsome Staffordshire bone china for its final journey to your hand-crafted solid-oak High Wycombe-bred table adorned with radiant white crisp Irish Linen spun from sun-ripened Erin flax and washed by colourful West Indian immigrants at the friendly neighbourhood Laundrama.'
Today most food descriptions are vulgar and inaccurate fantasies. We live in a world of garden peas that weren't

grown in a garden, farmhouse bread made by machine, home-made toffee from a trading estate, dairy ices from a giant freezing plant and farm butter manufactured in an industrial town.

Twenty hints on how to run
a bad restaurant

1   If you own the restaurant put in frequent appearances yourself. Stand at the back, slightly blocking the kitchen door, with a menacing look. A frown never did any harm. The busier and more over-worked the staff are the more important it is for you to resist the temptation to muck-in and help. Limit your interference to occasional teeth-clicking and 'tsks' of annoyance.

2   Remember, an un-cheery welcome doesn't cost you anything. Most of your clients will deserve nothing less. All that smiling and bowing and fawning foreigners get up to is most un-British. You should encourage your staff to be as icily correct as yourself. You set the standards, they will follow.

3   Try not to go out for your own meals when the restaurant is crowded. You never know when you'll be needed to sort out a trouble maker, there's one in every party. Hover round any table where revolt may be lurking and keep a close eye on the cutlery – some people will take the table as well if you don't keep them under constant scrutiny.

4   Ideally your premises should be hot and stuffy in summer and cold enough in winter to encourage customers to keep their outdoor clothes on. This will ensure that their stay is minimal.

5   Tables should be as close together as possible and of the smallest available size; eating out should be an intimate occasion. Make sure that your lighting is of the brightest – strong, overhead lighting enables you to see what everybody's up to and makes a dramatic effect when you start flicking the switches just before closing time.

6   Keep your opening hours as limited as possible. The staff may benefit indirectly but this cannot be helped. An ideal

time to serve lunches is 12.30 to 1 – keeping food hot after one is uneconomic and encourages people to take advantage of you. Don't forget, you are paying heavy rates and taxes, customers lounging about talking are abusing your hospitality.

7   The staff should be as few as possible. Ideally one person should do all the cooking and all the serving but this isn't always possible. Foreigners with no training and no knowledge of English make the best employees. If you have to have a British staff organize working conditions so that they are in a perpetual state of ferment. This unrest is quickly communicated to the customer which again makes for the shortest possible stay. Your ultimate aim should be to make every customer want to leave as quickly as possible.

8   Decorate the restaurant by all means, if you think it's worth it. Cardboard signs and advertisements are pleasant; so are plastic flowers which, however, are not at their best until they have been *in situ* for a good number of years. If you have to repaint the premises choose gay clashing colours.

9   If you provide toilet facilities – another millstone round your neck – ensure that they are inadequate. Your restaurant is a place to eat in not a comfort station. And remember a little bit of dirt never did anybody any harm.

10   Be wary of foreign tourists. They tend to ask for impossible things like fresh orange juice, glasses of water, green salads and ice. If you can do it without being too ingratiating head them off at the door, say you're fully booked, anything. Remember the best customer (not that there is such a thing as a good customer) is one who doesn't complain, i.e., a fellow Briton brought up in the same simple decent traditions as yourself.

11   Deal firmly with complaints. It is unfortunately not

possible for you or your staff to assault physically unruly elements but they should be given very short shrift indeed. Let your treatment of them be an object lesson to other diners. It's no good paying lip service to the rule that the customer is always wrong. Let him know.

12   Your customers will prefer to have their menu in English which is a good reason why you should put it in French. As only 3·2% of your clientele will understand even the most rudimentary French you can have an imposing *carte* without having an imposing *cuisine*. Although most people will know what a good beef stew should taste like, you can serve almost anything under the guise of a *ragoût*. Use French Creatively!

13   When planning your menus arrange to have the smallest number of portions of the largest number of dishes. This gives an impression of great variety but will enable the staff to cross most of the items off a few minutes after opening. Customers like to find things 'off' as it simplifies their choice.

14   Lukewarm food on cold plates, sodden chips, washed-out greens, over-cooked meat never did anybody permanent harm. If your cook is inclined to be slovenly or not very good at his job be patient. Remember there's no shortage of customers, there is a shortage of cooks.

15   Make sure that the portions are small and dainty. If you can get your materials tinned, frozen, dried, bottled or packeted, do so. Convenience foods are there for your convenience. Use them — exclusively if you can. There should be no need for a really intelligent caterer ever to meet his local butcher, baker, greengrocer or dairyman. Get your supplies from the factory – in bulk.

16   Don't forget the war-time slogan about not wasting food scraps. All your old vegetables and meat can be minced into

191

lovely croquettes, pasties, pies, rissoles or *vol-au-vents* (if you've got a classy trade). Re-heat, re-heat and re-heat until it's all gone. Remember the less in the swill the more in the till.

17   If you suspect members of the staff of being on the fiddle try and channel their competitive instincts where they will do the least harm – in the direction of the customer. A really decent customer doesn't quibble over small errors and mistakes in his bill.

18   Buy your wine cheaply and sell it expensively. The cheaper the wine the bigger the mark-up. People like to pay a lot for their wine, it gives them a sense of well-being and gives you a lot of profit for no work at all.

19   Charge as much as you can. Eating out for most folk is an experience. Make it a memorable occasion for them. Remember, too, the little extras that mean so much – cover charge, surcharge, service charge – we all have our own favourites.

20   Don't discourage your staff from stacking chairs on tables and sweeping up noisily as closing time approaches. Your customers would stay all night unless you gave them a mild hint

and

don't forget the golden rule

PEOPLE HAVE TO EAT SOMEWHERE